COME FEEL T

Ride 'Em C

"Everyone should read Dr. Sadie's books—they're life-changing."

—Barbara Leigh, *PLAYBOY*

"Dr. Sadie Allison combines sex education with erotic temptation so everyone can learn and enjoy. She's one of the great emerging sexologists of the 21st century."

—Dr. Ted McIlvenna, President,
The Institute for Advanced
Study of Human Sexuality

"Dr. Sadie Allison's writings have been a great resource for Cosmopolitan magazine throughout the world . . . her books have inspired me."

—Eleni Solomou,
Senior Editor & Columnist

"Dr. Sadie's sassy book gives you greater confidence to release your sexpot within and create new passions that thrill."

—Dr. Ava Cadell, Founder
of Loveology University®

RIDE 'EM COWGIRL!

RIDE 'EM COWGIRL!

Sex Position Secrets for Better Bucking

Dr. Sadie Allison

Illustrated by Steve Lee

ticklekitty®
Go love yourself.™
ticklekitty.com
SAN FRANCISCO

Dedicated to my Mom,

my biggest supporter and fan.

You are always in my heart.

I love you.

Tickle Kitty, Inc.
3701 Sacramento Street #107
San Francisco, CA 94118
United States
Fax: 1-(415) 876-1900
www.ticklekitty.com

Edited by Rich Lippman
Illustrated by Steve Lee
Interior design by Chris Hall/Ampersand
Cover design by Todd Gallopo/ Meat and Potatoes, Inc.
Cover and author photographs by Michael Bisco

PLEASE NOTE

Inside

ForePlay

Hi. How's sex lately?

If you and your lover can't keep your hands off each other, reveling in pleasures from head-to-toe, night and day, orgasm after orgasm, I know why you can't stop grinning.

Or maybe you're just grinning over fond memories.

How quickly our days of sexual frenzy become frenzied days of must-do's, need-to's and have-to's, with no time in between except for long-overdue sleep. When lovemaking does occur, it often waits for weekends, holidays, birthdays, anniversaries—even leap years!

Sex ruts happen, especially when couples stay together for months, years or decades. The good news: it's reversible.

So come on...I'm going to show you two lovebirds new ways to revive your passion and jumpstart a lot of that frenzied lovemaking once again!

And that's worth grinning about.

Welcome To Your Own Sexual Revolution

Ride 'Em Cowgirl! is different from every other sex position book you can find (and believe me, I've seen them all!). Here's why:

Instead of having to choose among hundreds of puzzling pretzel poses, I've shortened and organized the list to a handful of positions I'm sure you *already* love. I've then upgraded each one with orgasmic angle variations for pleasure-spot focus that you can easily adjust to fit your own unique shapes. Wait'll you try them!

I've kept everything fun, entertaining and inspiring for you, with over 100 illustrations by the incredible Steve Lee to help you visualize everything you may wish to try. And you'll never feel you've been left high and dry just before and after you orgasm: I've included lots of fun ways to stimulate your sexual appetite right up to *and during* penetration, along with passion-pleasing ideas to bring you gently back down (or up for another go-round!).

When I set out to write this guide, my goal was to empower women to take charge of their own sexual pleasures, to shake off self-defeating inhibitions, and to create their own magnificent orgasms, especially *during* penetration—a heart-racing joy too many women miss out on. I even named the book with *you-go-girl!* inspiration in mind for my female readers.

But *Ride 'Em Cowgirl!* is for guys too. After all, guys love women who revel in deep, orgasmic passion; who aren't shy about seducing with the visual power of their own naked bodies; who know what they want, when they want it, and how they want it.

Isn't that the whole point?

So this book is dual-purposed, featuring lots of pleasure tips just for "Cowgirls," along with another set of pleasure pointers for all you "Cowboys." After all, it takes two to tango, which is why this is truly a sexual empowerment guide for *couples.*

Cowgirls Only!
Be Empowered Now

As promised, this is the first of many sections for women only. Guys: *scram!* (Just kidding…this is your sneak peek into the other team's playbook. Feel free to read 'em all—just keep your jaw off the ground!).

Today, women want *and deserve* all the pleasures that are ours to claim. No longer is it simply a matter of waiting and hoping for good things to happen—now it's as straightforward as taking charge. And if you follow my prescription, sexual pleasure and magnificent orgasms will be yours for the taking. Ride 'em cowgirl!

Cowboys Only!
Just Give And You Shall Receive

As promised, this book is about *your* pleasure, too. It's a whisper in your ear about what your lover secretly wants, but isn't telling you. It's about opening exciting new communications between the two of you, both verbal and physical. And it's about discovering how being a generous lover brings back generous lovemaking in return. Ride 'em cowboy!

Cowgirls & Cowboys!
How To Fully Enjoy This Book

Do you ever wish your lover was a mind reader? Then you'd never have to overcome whatever stops you from asking for everything you desire during lovemaking.

I'm going to let you in on a little secret that'll not only inspire your partner to find and touch your erotic hot buttons—but also to lovingly kiss, tease, lick, caress, squeeze, stroke, nuzzle, spoon, tickle and cuddle them as well. Here's the secret:

Read this book *together*. In bed. Sit close and point at the fun stuff. Crease the corners. Giggle at the pictures. Then, when you open to those special erotic touches or lusty positions—the very ones you crave—your heart will quicken, your temperature will rise, you'll move in closer—and arousal, romance and passion will take over.

Congratulations! Your secret desire's out in the open—and you're already in bed. Now dive in while it's all so lusty and hot!

Laugh, learn, enjoy, be empowered—then empower each other.

X's and O's

Dr. Sadie

Dr. Sadie Allison

Important: Always practice safer sex—your life and health depend on it. Be sure to read, understand and apply everything in the Appendix on page 201 before engaging in any sexplay.

1 Your Passion Cocktail

Ever see monkeys making whoopie at the zoo, or dogs doing it doggystyle at the park?

Not exactly big on romance, are they?

That's what separates us from them. To most humans, the sex act is more than just a primal urge to merge. It's also an exotic cocktail of love, lust, passion, excitement, anticipation, desire, affection, romance and spice—with a splash of your own unique ingredients tossed in, too.

But how it's blended can mean all the difference between racing hearts—and raging heartburn.

So what's the best recipe for mixing the most potent passion cocktail? Easy! Tweak the ingredients. Add new spice. Leave out the bitters. Pop a cherry on top. Then shake well, pour with pride, open wide—and down you go!

Let's Get Physical

Are your best efforts in the sack producing hot'n'heavy breathing —or is that just a lot of huffing and puffing?

Whatever you do in life, you do it better when you're fit and healthy. That's especially true in lovemaking—a natural heart-pumping, lung-expanding, pore-opening workout. But is sex your *only* physical activity? C'mon! That eager person in bed with you is your lover—not your personal trainer!

Try using that free sidewalk outside your door for a brisk 20-minute walk every day. Or hop on a bicycle. Or join a gym. Even better, join a gym with your lover. You'll look great. You'll feel great. And you'll feel great to each other.

What's more, once you start exercising, the pleasure and intensity of your orgasms often get healthier, too. You'd think they'd print THAT on fitness center billboards!

Scoring Sex Etiquette Points

No one ever teaches you the finer points of sex etiquette. You either know it—or a disappointed lover lets you have it.

You can avoid this senseless humiliation by remembering and practicing *Dr. Sadie's Golden Rule of Sexual Passion:*

Do others as you would have them do you.

Please read that again…slowly.

Being a good lover is easier than many people realize, because the secret is as much about giving good orgasms as it is about everything that comes before and after, too. For instance…

 Clean up. Natural pheromone-y body scent is arousing; sweaty funk is not. Try to shower close to sex time, lathering up well in every crevice. Short on time? Spritz your pits with deodorant or try a light body spray. Don't forget to brush your teeth, and rinse with a minty mouthwash.

 Wash up. Dirty fingers don't belong in intimate areas. Wash your hands thoroughly with hot soapy water, file your nails smooth, and don't play with the dog on the way into the bedroom!

♥ **Groom up.** Are you growing a pubic jungle? Whether you're a trimmer, shape-shaver, clean-shaver, or somewhere in between, grooming minimizes trapped odors and looks stylish, too.

♥ **Spritz up.** Lightly scented perfumes and colognes can be a turn on—but too much tastes bad and can actually give your lover a headache.

Cowgirls Only!

How To Score Etiquette Points With Him

🐾 **Be penis friendly.** He's up for any attention—except icy-cold hands, jagged fingernails, hard dry-jerking, sharp teeth-scraping, zipper sideswiping, and hearing unfavorable comparisons to your ex-lovers!

🐾 **Ease up on yourself.** Try being less preoccupied with your not-so-perfect magazine-model body. After all, he isn't thinking about the size of your thighs—he's thinking about how good he'll feel inside you.

🐾 **Be snag-free.** The sensation of your jewelry against his skin can be a real turn-on. The exposed hooks and clasps that can snag and yank pubic hairs will be a real turn-off. Be careful!

🐾 **Open your mouth.** How will he know what you want if you don't tell him? (And he does want to know!) Just don't blurt it out like you're ordering a double latte—whisper it seductively into his ear, and seal it with a hot, wet, tongue-tip finish.

Cowboys Only!

Etiquette Points
Count Toward Fabulous Prizes!

🤠 **Shave yer shadow.** Your manly five o'clock stubble can feel like needles on your lover's face, breasts, thighs and especially her vulva. Don't risk irritating her. Slip a new blade in your razor and get as close as a man can get.

🤠 **Explore.** How does she like your touch: fast or slow, hard or deep, teasing or NOW? Spend more time getting to know her and show her you care—and feel the heat of passion come right back to you.

🤠 **Don't rush.** It's a scientific fact: a woman's body takes longer to warm up for intercourse than yours will. Spend more time exciting her body, and she'll reward you by spending more time exciting yours.

🌸 **Hold yer horses.** Resist the urge to place—or wrestle—her reluctant hand onto your burning crotch. She detests that almost as much as having her head shoved you know where….

🌸 **Cure your EDS.** That's Eager Dick Syndrome, where a huge, throbbing penis due out in the middle of the Second Act makes its grand entrance as the curtain rises. Keep it in your pants, Romeo, and savor the foreplay. She knows where it is.

🌸 **Juice up.** Nothing dampens a woman's mood more than premature, painful ramming with a dry finger or unlubricated penis. Start her juices flowing with your best foreplay, and slather on saliva or slippery sex lube before trying to insert anything.

🌸 **Angle in.** The delicate entrance to her vagina is not a funnel. Aim carefully when entering, and glide inside along the same angle as her vagina to avoid uncomfortable sideline poking—as well as keep you from slipping into the wrong orifice!

Dr. Sadie Sez: Are You Havin' A Laugh?
During sex, you're naked in more ways than one. You can greet the occasional slip-out, leg cramp, eye-poke, poot or queef with a grimace—or simply laugh it off together and continue on.

- 🤠 **Don't squash.** No matter how strong she may be, she shouldn't have to bench-press you! Spread your body weight across your knees, arms and elbows—not her chest. You want her to keep breathing, right?

Cowgirls & Cowboys!
Brighten Your Passion Picture

The big strokes of sex are easy—*anyone* can do them. But true passion is revealed in the fine strokes that turn lovemaking into an art. So which are you—a paint-by-the-numbers wannabe, or an original world-class artiste?

- ♥ **Kiss.** Why not spend more time enjoying some of the best sensations of sex? Savor all the heat you generate through deep, wet, soulful mouth-to-mouth kissing. Are you listening, longtime lovers?

- ♥ **Touch.** You already own a pair of the world's best sextoys: your hands! Each set includes 10 warm, eager fingers ready to caress, stroke, pinch, spank, tease, squeeze and please. No batteries required!

- ♥ **See.** Look into your lover's eyes and you gaze into your lover's soul. Keep your eyes locked during orgasm, and share this most intimate moment with your partner.

♥ **Listen.** The sounds of lovemaking are cues to your partner's state of arousal. Hot panting? Sensual moaning? Erotic screaming? Keep doing what you're doing. Sighing? Whining? Snoring? Try something else.

♥ **Talk.** Not about the weather—but about how turned on you are. Intimate talk during sex feels excitingly naughty, and can send your passions over the edge.

♥ **Ask.** "Does this feel good?" or "Do you like when I do this?" or "What would you like to try next?" Ask an exciting question and get an exciting answer.

♥ **Tease.** If you build sexual anticipation, you'll raise your lover's urgency for wilder sexual release. Try teasing before lovemaking, and feel new desires welling up deep inside.

♥ **Give.** When you're a generous lover, you think of your partner's pleasure before your own. When both of you are generous, the passion comes back to each of you, surging stronger with every lusty touch.

♥ **Savor.** Be patient! This isn't a race. Live in the moment. Try going in slow motion for a while before passions naturally speed things into a heated sexual frenzy.

2 Supergasms

An orgasm is an orgasm, right? Sure. And ice cream only comes in one flavor!

If you've "come" more than once in your life, you know how each orgasm can vary in intensity, character and duration. Climaxes often feel stronger when you're horny, softer when you're tired, and off-the-charts when you're tipsy, turned-on or crazy-in-love.

But what if you could supercharge ALL your orgasms? You'd not only amp up pleasure, you'd also lower your stress, burn more calories, ease menstrual cramps and enjoy deeper sleep—as well as plant an unwipeable smile on your face all day long.

This miracle is known as the mind/body connection—which simply means learning to be more in tune with yourself. And it all starts by knowing which sex organ is the biggest and most powerful.

The answer: your brain.

Cowgirls Only!
Are You Pre-Orgasmic?

> *Since most guys can orgasm in their sleep, this section is for every woman who has yet to orgasm, or would love to enhance orgasmic bliss.*

You do have the natural ability to orgasm—most every woman does. If you think you *might* have orgasmed, you probably haven't. If you can only orgasm on your own, but not with your partner, that doesn't mean you won't. There's lots of good news up ahead for you.

First, what *is* an orgasm, exactly? It's the climactic release of rising sexual excitement that you feel as a series of intensely euphoric and totally involuntary rhythmic pulsations throughout your vagina, uterus and rectum that can last as long *or longer* than it took you to read this entire sentence. And the next five words will actually help you experience them to the fullest: *teach yourself by touching yourself.*

> ### Dr. Sadie Sez: Be In The Here And Wow.
> It's hard to come when you're thinking about who's coming for dinner tomorrow. As tough as it might be, cast off your ongoing worries and stresses, no matter how often they creep in. Instead, savor *The Moment.* The scents. Sights. Sounds. Touch. Textures. Fantasy. Your lover's rising passion. And your own. Glorious orgasms await you…and are the best stress relievers in the world.

It's Okay To Get In Touch With Yourself

Universally endorsed by physicians and sex therapists—as well as orgasmic women around the world, gentle masturbation is the key to strengthening your mind/body connection, while opening up a new world of pleasure, excitement and well-being.

Here's the secret: Start by turning off the phones, tuning out your day, and maybe even drawing a hot, soothing bubble bath. Think sexy thoughts, perhaps about your lover, an old crush, a hunky movie star or even a forbidden acquaintance. Moisten a soft fingertip (or three!) with a few drops of slippery sex lubricant, then gently caress your clitoris while you squeeze your pelvic muscles in harmony with your fingertip motion. Vary your pressure, rhythm and touching styles till you find what feels best—then keep going. Now revel in all your satisfying feelings without straying from your lusty thoughts and fantasies.

It's okay if you don't orgasm for awhile—just get to know yourself by learning your private pleasure spots and discovering which stroking styles turn you on. Or try a small waterproof vibrator and feel it lift your pleasures! They're well-known for setting off countless first orgasms.

Once you experience your first glorious orgasm, you can now share your discovery with your lover, gently guiding his fingertips to the sensual new joys you've uncovered. For a complete guide on female masturbation techniques, send for a copy of *Tickle Your Fancy—A Woman's Guide to Sexual Self-Pleasure*, available in total confidence at *ticklekitty.com*.

If you are already orgasmic on your own, but not with your lover, try sharing the rest of this chapter with him, along with some of the delightful position variations throughout this book, and help him create the erotic clitoral contact you love during intercourse.

Dr. Sadie Sez: Rub-A-Dub-Tub.

One of the most popular ways women learn to achieve their first orgasm is in the tub. Place your hips under the flow of warm water for clitoral pleasures, or aim a jet of warm water from a handheld showerhead to open up to pleasureful sensations.

Cowgirls Only!
The Male Orgasm Menu

Understanding your partner's orgasm is one sign of a generous lover, and knowing how to supercharge it is yet another. Did you know your guy can experience *two* different kinds of orgasms?

- **Penis Os.** The most widely known male orgasm is triggered at the top of the penis, where thousands of erotic nerves cluster at the head. To bring out the most pleasure, treat this area to your most sensual rhythmic friction at the pace he desires, along with some deliciously slippery wetness.

- **Prostate Os.** The alternate male orgasm trigger is his prostate gland, located behind the base of the penis, and reachable through his anus. The best sensations are achieved with direct stimulation using a finger or sextoy, together with heavenly penis stimulation from your hand and mouth. See more in chapter 12.

Cowboys Only!
The Art Of The Female Orgasm

Imagine your lover's soft, warm, slippery fingers giving you a world-class handjob, but only to the *bottom half* of your penis.

How long before you'd go out of your mind?

It's the same for your partner. She needs the same loving touch that you crave (and more!) in one special place: on or around her clitoris!

And with clitoral, vaginal, G-spot, multiple and liquid orgasms in her pleasure trove, your focus on how and where you touch determines whether she'll go out of her mind with pleasure—or frustration. The difference often comes down to one small word: *Ask*.

Simply checking in with her about what she likes will show you're truly a generous lover who's unafraid to ask for directions.

Come...Meet The Clitoris

The clitoris is the only human organ designed purely for pleasure, and, sorry gentlemen, it's a woman-only advantage. But we *will* let you play with it!

Here's one good reason: it's loaded with millions of the same orgasm-triggering nerve endings as in your penis, only they're packed into an area the size of a pea!

Some women prefer soft, indirect caressing. Others love rapid, direct touching. And some crave both, depending on how near they are to orgasm. Remember, if you aren't sure how your lover likes

to be touched, *ask!* She may only be able to come if you stimulate her clitoris the way she likes it.

Once you're tuned in to her perfect touch, you can then tailor the angles of your positions and motions to deliver the hottest erotic friction to her clitoris. To find out more about star-quality clitoral contact, you need look no further than chapter 9!

The Female Orgasmic Combo Platter

How many different ways can a woman orgasm? Let us count the ways…

- **Clitoral Os.** Clitoral caressing is your path to her Big O. Vary the pressure, speed and stroke of your fingertip-touch till you find what melts her into orgasmic bliss. Respond to her non-verbal cues and ask her what feels good. Then apply this powerful carnal knowledge to your position angles and penetration motions during intercourse.

- **Vaginal Os.** While vaginal orgasms are technically possible without any direct clitoral stimulation, the clitoris usually receives *indirect* erotic stimulation during penetration, with the penis pushing and pulling on the inner labia, which tugs and tantalizes the clitoris, too. Expand your lover's orgasmic potential by including more deliberate clitoral stimulation, instead of hoping for indirect success.

- **G-spot Os.** These deeper, longer, more body-wide orgasms can be your lover's when you stimulate her G-spot just right. Her G-spot will usually be even more responsive after one or two clitoral orgasms, followed by continuing clitoral pleasure together with G-spot simulation. Find out more: see chapter 10 for the ins and outs.

- **Multiple Os.** If your lover's rest time between orgasms is measured in minutes—or seconds—she has a gift for multiple orgasms. It's a team effort to bring them on: shortly after she comes, you begin gentle clitoral stimulation as she squeezes and holds her pelvic muscles tight, thinking about the joy of another orgasm. It'll feel like she's between a sensitive breath-taking delight and an almost unbearable "ticklish" sensation as she reaches for another orgasm…and another!

- **Liquid Os.** One of the most powerful full-body pleasures of all, "female ejaculation" most often occurs during a G-spot orgasm, causing a rush of clear liquid from the urethra, which is not urine, and perfectly normal. In fact, most women and men find it highly arousing! Read more about the power of liquid orgasms in chapter 10.

Supersize Your HE-gasms!

Because orgasms feel so good and happen so naturally, it's easy to just accept what comes. Till now, perhaps?

- **Stronger Os.** You can easily bulk-up your "orgasm muscle" for greater pleasures—and send your ejaculate flying further! Just try a simple exercise during halftime, lunchtime or drivetime, and soon, at the moment of orgasm, squeeze your strengthened orgasm muscle for an explosive result! Want to try? Turn to the next page.

- **Longer Os.** Get to know your orgasmic "trigger point"—as well as the instant just before that point of no return when you can still hold back. As it nears, stop stroking (or pull out) and relax your body till the feeling vanishes—then start up again. Repeat this technique (aka "edging") several times, so when you finally let yourself explode, your orgasm should last longer than ever!

- **Multiple Os.** If you wish to pick up again without the usual downtime in between orgasms, learn to orgasm without ejaculating. The difference? Orgasm is the pleasurable feeling of climax, while ejaculation is the actual fluid release. Practice combining the stronger and longer techniques above to achieve Multiple Os.

- **Simultaneous Os.** Coming together isn't a requirement for great sex—but it is great! By learning your partner's sexual responses, you can time yourself to hold back and climax with her. Since women can take at least three times longer to orgasm, stimulate her with lots of foreplay, as well as a clitoral orgasm

or two before intercourse. If she communicates her excitement with a heated cry of *"I'm coming!"*— you can let go at the right moment and come together. It doesn't come easy, but what fun you'll have trying!

Cowgirls & Cowboys!
Strengthen Your Orgasm Muscle!

If you *really* have to pee, but there's no bathroom in sight, the muscle you must squeeze to hold it in is called your Pubococcygeus muscle, (a.k.a. the PC or pelvic muscle). In women and men, the PC muscle stretches from the anus, across the pelvic region to the pubic bone, and it's what you feel contracting involuntarily during orgasm, creating those indescribable waves of sexual pleasure.

Now that you know where it is, what it does, and how to flex it, why not learn how to strengthen it? The power of your orgasms depends on it!

PC muscle toning exercises are called Kegels (KAY-gulls), which are simply the act of squeezing and releasing these muscles. Begin a good habit of doing Kegels when you have a few spare moments, like waiting at red lights. They're best performed on an empty bladder, and not during urination. Here's an excellent daily toning-and-tightening workout:

1. Clench your PC muscle tight, and hold for 4 seconds.
2. Unclench for 3 seconds.
3. Repeat 10 times.
4. Perform a total of 5 sets over the course of each day.

Breathe steadily, and clench *only* your PC muscle—not your butt or stomach muscles. Go ahead, try it now—even if you're in the middle of a bookstore.

Successful toning can lead you to enjoy longer, stronger, more frequent, multiple or first orgasms! In women, it can help rejuvenate vaginal tightness after childbirth, or offer a new grip if you're sleeping with a less-than-girthy lover. For men, it can help reverse erectile dysfunction and premature ejaculation. Results may take several weeks, but keep at it—the improvement can be dramatic.

Dr. Sadie Sez: Ladies, Be A Super-Kegeler!

For faster progress, try using Kegel exercise products specifically designed to help you strengthen your orgasm muscle.

3 The Art of Penetration

Cowgirls: Skip ahead to chapter 4, or read on if you dare.

Ahhh. . . Those first frenzied moments when penis touches labia. When every sexual sensory cell yearns to be stroked. When the thrill of conquest is on the verge of being rewarded. When the primal need to plunge propels you forward into slippery-hot tightness.

There's a real art to intensifying these feelings of penetration for you and your lover—and you're the artist.

But knowing she will experience these first few moments of ecstasy differently from you is key to creating your masterpiece.

What does she crave? How can you supercharge it? Come probe.

Wetness: The Lube of Love

It probably goes against every bone in your body—especially that big throbbing one—but unless your woman tells you she wants it hard and fast right from the get-go, resist the lust to thrust.

Why? She's not ready.

Your lover won't feel very loving if you start trying to penetrate before she's fully preheated. It's boorish, selfish, and can be uncomfortable or even painful for her. *Remember:* If she's dry, standby. If she's wet, you're all set.

Treat Her To An Exotic Labial Massage

This massage isn't on the menu at any spa—but add it to *your* menu and she could flow like a fountain.

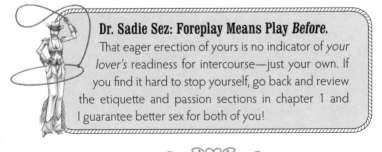

Dr. Sadie Sez: Foreplay Means Play *Before.*

That eager erection of yours is no indicator of *your lover's* readiness for intercourse—just your own. If you find it hard to stop yourself, go back and review the etiquette and passion sections in chapter 1 and I guarantee better sex for both of you!

> ### Dr. Sadie Sez: A Sex Lube to Drool For.
> No lube handy? You always have a ready supply of saliva. While it works, it's also short-lived and will stop being slippery very quickly. Be sure to reapply often, or the dry friction will ruin your pleasure play. Better yet, always keep a bottle of quality sex lube nearby—and apply it generously.

Here's how: drizzle a little sex lube or saliva directly into the action and spread it around, so you're both glistening and slippery.

With your hand, slowly guide the head of your slippery erect penis right up to the entrance of her vagina. *Resist the urge to go deep!* Instead, slowly tease by circling the tip all around the opening, then glide it between her labia up to her clitoris. After a few tempting clitoral swirls, slide it back down to the opening.

Repeat your special massage with several more sensual laps up and down her labia. Admire the view, enjoy the sensations, don't rush, and use all your superpowers to stay outside. Your rewards will soon come.

Making Your Grand Entrance

When you can't wait any longer, use your hand to help slide the head of your penis inside. Feel her soft lips surround you as you stimulate those millions of pleasure cells at the mouth of her vagina.

But now's not the time to go on autopilot—use your sixth sense to match the angle of your erection to her angle of acceptance. Start slowly, and if all is well, go a little deeper, then deeper, then deeper till you're completely inside.

This is what many women fondly call the "hurts so good" moment—when the vagina is spread wider with pleasure by your grand penetration and the thrilling feeling of fullness. If your lover is expressive, you'll hear all about it in her sensual vocalizations.

Now you're faced with a choice. You can start pounding in'n'out like every other Tom, Harry and Dick—or you can thrill her with some incredible sensual abilities, which is exactly what she wants!

Get Your Pump On

By nature, the male always has some (or most) control over the pumping. So why limit yourself to driving in just one gear?

- **Head Bob.** To tease her into a yearning frenzy, stroke shallowly, in'n'out, with just the head of your penis for awhile, nothing deeper.

- **Combo Platter.** Try three mini-pumps only a few inches inside, followed by one long, deep, graceful thrust. Repeat in rhythm.

- **Divine Grind.** Show her you know her by grinding your cushy pubic bone into her tender clitoris…slowly…sensually…erotically …while your penis fills her.

- **Knead To Speed.** After a slow, teasing start, accelerate your pumping toward orgasm. If you feel like you're going to come too soon, downshift and try the Divine Grind.

- **Angle The Dangle.** Your mission: find ALL your lover's internal pleasure spots. Pivot and angle your penis all around till she moves and moans with pleasure.

- **Love Lever G.** With your penis buried inside, angle and position for targeted G-spot stroking. To line up your target, see chapter 10.

- **Jackhammer.** Some women love it hard and fast. Some don't know till they try it. And the rest will never like it. So try it once— and if she goes crazy with delight, keep drilling!

- **Rhythm Nation.** There's a reason sex is known as horizontal dancing—it's the rhythm. Rather than pump mechanically— groove to the excitement of making love together, pumping, grinding and gyrating in synch with your mutual passion as your entire bodies sway in harmony, including hips, shoulders and knees.

Secrets To Being
Her *Sexiest* Pleasure Partner

Whether this is brand new to you, or merely a refresher course, the biggest thrills of sex are now in your capable hands:

- Run the warm wet tip of your tongue up her neck, slowly and seductively to her ear, then halfway down. Add in a few angel kisses and exhale lightly to excite her now-moistened skin.

- Try gentle hair-pulling, pinching, spanking, scratching, tickling, tossing, chasing, loving, wrestling in the nude. Be creative and surprise each other!

- Engage those living sextoys also known as hands! Feel your sexual energy flow through your fingers wherever you touch, from her hair to her feet.

- Kiss like a rock star. With all your soul. Every time.

- Lick like a movie star. Nibble, kiss, bite and tug all over her luscious body—especially her highly sensitive nipples.

- Think of your penis as a multi-function pleasure device with variable speeds and lots of factory options—not simply a one-speed jackhammer.

Dr. Sadie Sez:
Four Ways To GUARANTEE Super Sex.
- ♥ Be attuned to her body—with ALL your senses.
- ♥ Go slow—this isn't rush hour.
- ♥ Be clitoris-cunning—touch, tease, titillate, tantalize.
- ♥ Practice sex safely—all the time.

♣ Treat her natural lube like rare nectar—gently glide your fingertips over her glistening labia and spread her lube all over her most arousable spots.

♣ Instead of heading directly into the heat of the action, try teasing her inner thighs and everywhere BUT her vagina till it glistens and aches to be touched.

♣ Squeeze, cup, knead and draw her butt closer to you as you enter her—and with every breathtaking stroke.

♣ Does she like to be "taken?" Try grasping both her hands, and pin them down on the bed over her head. Now grind slowly inside as you nibble on her ear lobes and whisper naughty words.

♣ While you're deep inside her, flex your PC muscles and arouse her with a surprising heartbeat sensation. Go to page 18 and see how to get good at it!

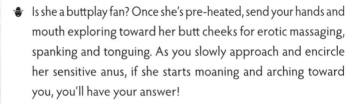

- Is she a buttplay fan? Once she's pre-heated, send your hands and mouth exploring toward her butt cheeks for erotic massaging, spanking and tonguing. As you slowly approach and encircle her sensitive anus, if she starts moaning and arching toward you, you'll have your answer!

- Are you at half-mast? Never try to shoehorn your penis inside and pray for wood. Take a break and enjoy lots of erotic fun while bringing yourself back to hardness. Use your hands and mouth and enjoy *her* pleasure.

- What's her fetish? You don't know? Try exploring, probing and asking to find out if there are any beneath the surface just waiting to explode. And wait'll you see how wild she gets when you uncover her sexual secrets!

- Out of breath? Take a break—this isn't a marathon. Nibble on chocolate, sip some water, catch your breath. Then get back to business.

Whisper. Moan. Or Wake The Neighborhood!

Usually, good sex isn't so quiet. For some, it's even more exciting when others may be listening. But the natural sounds of sex don't have to be loud—just thrilling.

- **Language.** Often the right words at the right time can trigger an orgasmic volcano. Tell her how sexy she is, how good she smells, how hot she makes you feel. Maybe she'll follow your lead.

- **Talk dirty.** Here's where you finally get to say all those really dirty words, but in the right context. If your lover can handle it, look her in the eye and tell her exactly what you're going to do to her.

- **Ejaculations.** Not the liquid kind, but the verbal kind! Instead of words, guide her to what feels good with moans, sighs, deep breathing, loud *ohhhhs* and long sensual *aaaaaaahhhhs*.

- **Listen closely.** Her vocalizations are clues to what she likes (and what she doesn't). Take her verbal cues and set off some fireworks. And if you hear her moan, "Just like THAT. *Yes!* Right *there*. Don't stop!"—then don't stop—no matter what!

- **Ask.** It's okay to use words to discover her physical cravings. Say, "Does this feel good?" or "Should I rub a little harder?" Then do exactly what she wants.

Cork Poppers Anonymous

If concentrating on the rules of baseball or mentally reciting the Pledge of Allegiance is your secret way to keep from coming too quickly, perhaps you'd like to find a better way.

- **Stop pumping.** Try the Divine Grind, keeping the head of your penis as still as you can.

- **Withdraw slowly.** Wait till the feeling subsides—but keep stimulating her.

- **Change positions.** Use the out-time for kissing, light spanking and even some clitoral licking.

- **Try a ring.** Wear a penis ring to slow the approach of orgasm, as well as increase its intensity (unless you have heart problems or diabetes).

- **Exercise.** Bulk up your PC muscle, which will give you greater control over your orgasm trigger.

- **Stay sober.** Lay off the alcohol and drugs. These dull the self-awareness you need to recognize and pull back before that point-of-no-return.

- **Wrap up.** Wear a condom—they're not just for safer sex and birth control.

- **Be comfortably numb.** Try applying a topical numbing cream to desensitize the head of your penis.

4 The Art Of Being Penetrated

Cowgirls Only!

Cowboys: Come spy on the other team's playbook.

Ahhh... Those first glorious moments as penis touches vagina. When every sexual sensory cell yearns to be caressed. When labia blossom like a delicate flower, enticing him inside. When the need for that exquisite feeling of fullness stimulates a deep, deep passion within.

There's an art to intensifying these divine feelings of penetration for both you and your lover—and you're the artist. But knowing he will experience these first few moments differently from you is the key to creating your masterpiece.

What does your lover crave? How can you heighten your own pleasure? Try any or all of these erotic moves, and feel passions rise.

Wetness: The Lube Of Love

Most guys are ready for sex at hello, which probably explains why yours may be eager to start thrusting long before you're ready. This should come as no surprise—he's genetically programmed that way.

But *you* must be physically ready, too. This means being totally, wonderfully, sensually lubricated.

If he starts his move to mount, and you're still dry or only a little moist, let him know you're not ready and continue foreplay until you're naturally lubricated. Or simply reach for the sex lube and drizzle sensual slipperiness around your vagina and all over his penis. Remember: *no glide—no ride!*

You've Got To Hand It To Yourself

What could feel better than your partner's able hand gliding the fleshy head of his penis sensually around your labia and clitoris?

YOUR hand in command.

Dr. Sadie Sez: All Out Of Sex Lube?

Then try saliva, the spreadable lube always on the tip of your tongue. While it can work well, it doesn't last too long. So reapply as needed, or the dry friction will quickly ruin your pleasure play. Better yet, always keep a bottle of quality sex lube nearby—and apply it generously.

Slip your fingers and thumb gently around his penis, and glide its head over your lips and clitoris the way *you* like it. (If he's paying attention, he'll remember your pleasure pattern for next time.) If a little more wetness would feel a whole lot better, drizzle on some sex lube and revel in the slippery sensations. Take your time, create your pleasures, and you'll zoom toward exotic new orgasms together.

Make His Entrance A Grand One

Once you're ready, tilt your hips so the slope of your vagina complements his angle of erection. Off-angle penetration, even with plenty of lube, can be uncomfortable. But a harmonious slide inside always takes your breath away.

If you're on top, be a bit of a tease: slide only the tip of his penis in and out to awaken the millions of pleasure cells at the entrance of

your vagina. Then stop moving and give him a few loving squeezes with your PC muscles (and watch his eyes bulge out of his head).

Deepen the tease by easing him inside slowly (next time, when he thinks he knows what's coming, surprise him with one swift graceful push to the hilt). Then, on your every slow, agonizing out-stroke, squeeze his erection tight—or keep him fully submerged at your ideal angle for clitoral gyrating—and let nature take over.

Get Your Pump On

By nature's design, most everything feels good to him once he's inside you. But you can turn "good" into *goodness-gracious-great-balls-of-fire!* Here's how:

🐞 **Head Bob.** Try stroking only the head of his penis inside the entrance to your vagina, in'n'out, over and over, till he *must have* all of you.

🐞 **Combo Platter.** Follow three luscious Head Bobs with one long, deep, graceful thrust. Repeat in rhythm.

🐞 **Love Lever G.** When he's inside you, angle yourself so his penis probes your G-spot. To line up your pleasure spot, see chapter 10.

Dr. Sadie Sez: Play To His Orgasm Trigger.

Sweeten the pace of sex by adjusting your penetration style. If your lover's got staying power, congratulations! And when you're ready to wrap it up, try the Combo Platter on the opposite page to bring him to a rousing finish. If he's got a hair-trigger, try the Divine Grind (below) to minimize friction to the head of his penis, while you enjoy delicious clitoral stimulation. Your mileage may vary, so keep experimenting till you find which strokes work best.

🕷 **Divine Grind.** While on top, don't be shy about rubbing your clitoris into his cushiony pubic area, and taking control of your own pleasure while giving him deep thrills.

🕷 **Knead To Speed.** After a slow, teasing start, begin accelerating your pumping to fast 'n' furious as his orgasm nears—being sure you stay well-aligned so you don't hurt his penis! Or, if you started at jackhammer speed, slow it down for his grand finale, pumping with long, luxurious thrusting.

🕷 **Deep Gulp.** Try imagining your vagina as a warm, wet mouth determined to swallow and suck his erection with every delicious stroke. Grip and squeeze him on the way in, then release him on the way out—or vice versa! To strengthen your grip, see page 18.

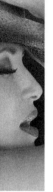

♨ **Flower Show.** Since your guy craves erotic visuals, try this: When you're on top, spread open your labia with your fingertips, and let him watch his penis go in and out of you. Complete the erotic picture by licking your lips, playing with your breasts, arching your back, tossing your hair. He'll be on Cloud Nine.

♨ **Rhythm Nation.** There's a reason sex is known as horizontal dancing—it's the rhythm. Rather than pump mechanically— groove to the excitement of your lovemaking, pumping, grinding and swirling your hips in synch with your mutual passions as your entire bodies sway in harmony, including hips, shoulders and knees. Play your favorite CD.

Secrets To Being His *Sexiest* Pleasure Partner

Whether this is brand new to you, or merely a refresher course, the biggest thrills of sex are now in your capable hands:

♨ During the walk to the car, in a darkened theater, or on the ride home, lean over and whisper, "I'm not wearing any panties." You'll rock his world.

♨ Bring your favorite sextoys into bed with you. It's good to share, and he may like it more than you think.

🐸 Play to his visual fantasies with props, wigs and outfits. Dress up like a sexy prostitute, horny school teacher or runaway nun. Then gaze deeply into his eyes, give him hot "come hither" looks, run your tongue over your lips and touch yourself all over. This is no time to be shy!

🐸 Don't bypass his sensitive nipples. Just figure out whether he likes them nibbled, sucked, licked, tugged, pinched—or all of the above.

🐸 Engage your living sextoys—your hands! Suck on your fingers, then place them on his lips to be sucked. Send them exploring into sensitive crevices. Be imaginative!

🐸 To race stimulation into high gear, reach over and caress his balls like they're two delicate eggs. Or massage his butt and tease his anus.

🐸 To slow a too-quick orgasm, try recreating a penis ring by encircling the base of his penis with your thumb and forefinger and squeezing firmly.

🐸 Time for a new position? Don't wait for him to decide. Take charge and realign your bodies—even better if it's a position you two have never tried!

> **Dr. Sadie Sez:**
> **Four ways To GUARANTEE Super Sex.**
> ♥ Be expressive—steer him to your hotspots with whispers and moans.
> ♥ Be enthusiastic—raise the heat with some new erotic confidence.
> ♥ Be generous—give in bed and ye shall receive in bed.
> ♥ Practice sex safely—all the time.

♣ When you're on the bottom, wrap your legs around hi hips and *pull* him into you. Gyrate just how YOU like it, with circles and arches that create the angles you love.

♣ Will he go for buttplay? Find out: send your hands and mouth inching toward his butt cheeks for erotic massaging, tonguing and even spanking. If he starts moaning and arching toward you as you slowly approach and encircle his sensitive anus, you'll have your answer!

♣ Feeling voyeuristic? Try a few strategically placed mirrors around the room for a front-row seat to your own lovemaking. See how erotic it is to watch your lover's every in-out thrust as he penetrates you. More beautiful than you thought? Now you know why guys are so visual.

🧘 Out of breath? Take a break—this isn't a marathon. Nibble on chocolate, sip some water, catch your breath. Then get back to business.

Why Silence Is Not Golden

If sex is starting to sound like a night at the library, perhaps it's time to start opening your mouths for a new reason…

🧘 **Language.** Often the right words at the right time can send your lover into overdrive. Whisper how sexy he is, how much you want him, how hot he makes you, and if you love him, why not tell him?

🧘 **Talk dirty.** Between two lovers, dirty talk at the height of passion can ignite a true orgasmic firestorm. You may feel the bonds of upbringing holding you back, but it can also feel liberating to let them go. Look him in the eye, and in a breathless whisper say, "I am *so* wet for you!" or "I want to ride you, BAD," or "Lick my tits!" Then watch him race into high gear. For real fireworks, when you reach that point-of-no-return, scream out, "I'm coming!"

🧘 **Express yourself.** Instead of words, let him know how good he makes you feel with sex sounds. This will also guide him to

keep doing what he's doing. Let your low moans, deep breathing, shake-the-rafters *ohhhhs* and long sensual *aaaaaaahhhhs* be the soundtrack of your growing arousal.

🐞 **Listen.** His vocalizations are clues to what he likes (and what he doesn't). And if you hear him moaning, "Just like THAT. *Yes!* Right *there.* Don't stop!"—then don't stop—no matter what!

🐞 **Ask.** It's okay to find out what he's craving by coyly asking, "Does this feel good?" or "Should I rub a little harder?" If you don't open your mouth, you run the risk of wondering, "Am I doing this right?" or "Does he even like what I'm doing?"

🐞 **Talk sex.** That's right, but not just when you're in bed. Candid discussions *out* of the heat of passion can lead to much hotter passion later.

5 Missionary Possible

Humankind owes a great big thank you to Mother Nature. After all, how many four-legged creatures will ever experience the thrill of face-to-face intercourse, *ohhhing* and *aahhing* into each other's furry ears?

Yet for us two-legged upright types, Missionary is one of the most natural positions of all—a perfect complement to our human physique as well as our mutual angles of penetration. Perhaps that's why it's the best starter position for budding lovers, easily solving those sticky first-time *who-goes-how-and-where* situations.

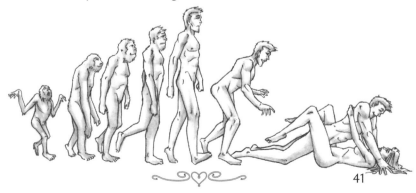

Regardless of its puzzling and totally un-sexy name, Missionary stands as one of Mother Nature's proudest evolutionary achievements. Think of it as her loving gift to you.

Your Mission: Make It Even Better

By treating Missionary as a thrilling journey rather than an everyday commute, you demonstrate what drives true erotic creativity.

When you spread out the pull of gravity over your bodies, you're free to explore with your fingers, lips, tongue, eyes and ears. Slide a moistened fingertip or three into your lover's most arousable spots. Press your mouths together in a hot, wet kiss to simulate your hot, wet penetration down below. Tune your ears to the faintest whispers and moans escaping your lover's lips. Lock eyes as passions rise and revel in your lover's private orgasm face.

Then, just when you think it can't get any better, try some of the lusty position variations illustrated for you in this chapter.

Limbs: Your Levers Of Love

You don't have to hang from the rafters to experience wild new sensations—simply fine tune your angles of penetration for stronger orgasms. But instead of just re-aiming your penis or vagina, try

adjusting the mechanics of your arms and legs for surprising new pleasures.

♥ **Access.** When the woman bends her knees and spreads them outward, the man gains deeper access to stimulate her clitoris with his fleshy pubic area, as well as penis-stroke her G-spot.

♥ **Depth.** When she raises her legs, his penis can plunge even deeper. If she places her knees in his armpits, or her legs over his shoulders, or her legs high over her head, the dramatic new angles can lead to dramatic new orgasms. To maximize comfort, play to the relative length of your penis-to-vagina fit (they both grow as arousal heightens). *Caution: Never plunge too deep too fast, since pain or injury can occur to the cervix at the end of the canal.*

♥ **Friction.** When she extends her legs straight, and he places his legs outside hers, he can grind into her clitoris as she grips him with her tightened vagina. Score extra points if there's no "slip out" during the switch! *Caution: Trim pubic hair around the vaginal lips (labia) to avoid irritating the base of his penis.*

♥ **Closeness.** When she wraps her legs behind his back, she can pull him closer for intimate grinding on her clitoris. He can enhance the effect by rocking and rolling rather than thrusting.

Cowboys Only!

Hip! Hip! Excitement!

Try resisting the urge to buck like a wild pornstar. Instead, think of your hips as a powerful locomotive—with you at the controls.

- **Swooper Man.** Swivel your hips down and around till you find what feels good. Then tuck your pelvis under during each up-swoop. Be sure there's plenty of lube to smooth your moves.

- **Grinder Guy.** Sink your penis deep inside and grind your fleshy pubic mound into her clitoris (this may even help you extend pleasure by slowing down your orgasm). Then pull back just far enough to slide your slippery fingertip onto her excited clitoris.

- **Side Winder.** Try some gentle side-to-side motions as you thrust in, beginning when your penis is about two-thirds of the way inside.

- **Pleasure Cocoon.** With both your bodies fully extended, wrap your arms tightly around each other. As you support your weight on your elbows, feel the ultimate physical connection two human beings can feel. Now rock your hips in perfect harmony and experience supreme bliss as you approach orgasm together.

Dr. Sadie Sez: Discover The Power Push.
Try turbo-charging your thrusting: gain extra leverage by placing your feet on the headboard, baseboard, bed frame, dresser, wall—or dashboard.

- **Coochie Lift.** Place a small pillow under her hips to give her just enough elevation for that extraordinary angle of acceptance that brings focused pleasures all along your penis and throughout her vagina.

Cowgirls Only!
Don't Bottom Out

While your range of motion on the bottom may be limited, don't just lie there! Thrust up to meet his eager thrusts down. Swivel your hips and feel the rush of his penis in new and exciting ways. Grip him vaginally every time he plunges inside. Brace your hands on the bed or headboard for extra thrusting power. Then reach around and gently tantalize his balls, or slip your hot little fingertip onto his puckered, unsuspecting anus—and hold on tight.

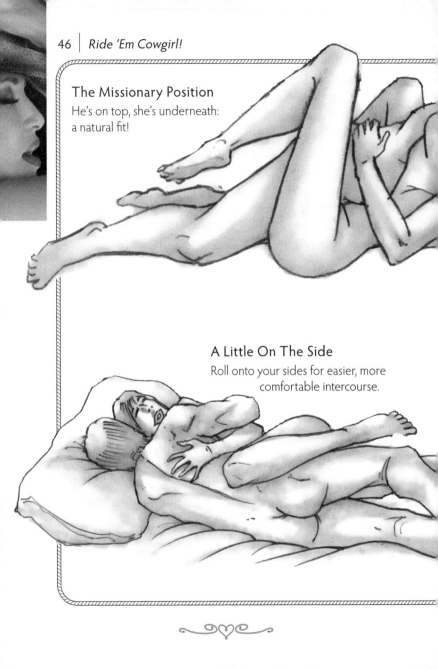

The Missionary Position

He's on top, she's underneath:
a natural fit!

A Little On The Side

Roll onto your sides for easier, more
comfortable intercourse.

The Nutcracker

Probe for all your perfect pleasure spots by re-adjusting your knees, elbows and hands.

The Plow

Deep and sexy, with G-spot pleasures and clitoral gyrations, too. Try licking and kissing her toes!

The Jellyroll

Deep exploration with
erotic body views, as
both of you push and pull
in orgasmic harmony.

Deep Mission
Lusty kissing and eye-gazing with ultra-deep penetration. Careful... go deep gradually.

The Bare Hug
By locking her ankles around his waist, she can pull him deeper and stimulate her clitoris just how she likes it.

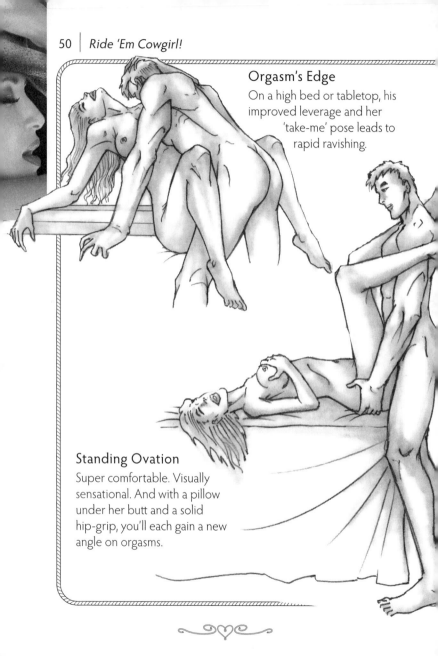

Orgasm's Edge

On a high bed or tabletop, his
improved leverage and her
'take-me' pose leads to
rapid ravishing.

Standing Ovation

Super comfortable. Visually
sensational. And with a pillow
under her butt and a solid
hip-grip, you'll each gain a new
angle on orgasms.

Lean Machine

A long, lean, sexy look for her to savor, plus bouncing breasts for him to watch. How good would it feel if she reached under to play with his balls?

Kneel 'n' Squeal

Deep penetration with deeper G-spot joys. Raise her butt with a small pillow for an entirely new sensation. Now…which of you will fingertip her clitoris?

6 Doggystyle

There's only one expression that accurately captures the primal passion of orgasmically explosive, testicle-swinging, rear-entry doggystyle sex.

"Bow **WOW!**"

Think about it. While she's relishing the deepest penetration, the most heavenly G-spot stimulation, and the animalistic excitement of being taken from behind—he's reveling in the world's most erotic visuals, stem-to-stern penis pleasure, and the primal satisfaction of sexual conquest.

And you're just getting started.

With an array of pleasure angles for her to play, and many more lusty moves at his command, Doggystyle can ignite red-hot sexual passion like no other position.

So don't be fooled by its bonehead name. Just find what works best for you—and be glad wagging tails never get in the way!

Cowboys Only!
Raise Your Pleasure IQ

Being on top doesn't always make you top dog. But these moves will:

- **Freehand treats.** Your hands and mouth are free to roam, so send 'em exploring. Kiss and nuzzle her neck and shoulders. Toss her hair—or pull it. Caress her breasts and tease her nipples. Run your fingers down her back, then slap her butt. You'll quickly find out what she likes, and *how* she likes it.

- **Clitoral treats.** Reach around to gently fingertip her clitoris in synch with your thrusting. This position is very comfortable on your hand and wrist, so you can stimulate her all the way to orgasm—maybe even orgasm together!

- **Anal treats.** At your fingertip, one of her hottest pleasure spots beckons. Gently massage her inner butt cheeks, inching

your fingers slowly toward the sensitive center. Without slowing intercourse, touch one lubricated fingertip lightly on her anus. Is she going bonkers? Slowly send your finger inside—but only to the first knuckle—and hold it perfectly still. Is she going wild? Send your finger a little deeper, and start stroking in'n'out in harmony with your penis. Try a little wiggling, too. This double stimulation can launch her biggest orgasms! *Note:* Once you've touched her anus, those fingers cannot touch her vagina until you've thoroughly washed your hands with antibacterial soap and water.

- **G-spot treats.** With her body turned a full 180 degrees "upside-down" from Missionary and Cowgirl, your penis enters her on a path to her G-spot. By varying your angle of entry slightly, you can stroke it directly (if you're not sure, ask "Does that feel good?"). Once you've found the bull's-eye, sway your hips in mini-circles (instead of in'n'out), burrowing the head of your penis into her G-spot. You could give her the most powerful G-spot orgasm ever. Learn more in chapter 10.

- **Pavlov's treats.** It's the most stimulating sight on earth to see her soft butt bouncing on your thrusting hips…to feel your penis penetrating her so deeply…to hear her excited orgasmic moaning…to feel your testicles slapping to the beat—*no wonder* you get off so quickly. To put off orgasm a little longer, try holding still insider her while you gently fingertip her clitoris. When she's ready to come, so are you!

Cowgirls Only!

Arch, Angle And Play For Pleasure

You'll be amazed what a few small adjustments can mean to both of you:

🌟 **Arch yourself.** Would you prefer his penetration deeper or shallower? To send him deepest, arch your back, lower your chest and spread your legs wider (delicious eye-candy for him!). To keep him shallower, flatten your arch till your hips are tucked down and under. Slowly adjust your arch till you find the depth that feels best, or rotate it up and down throughout your lovemaking.

🌟 **Angle yourself.** To find your own "WOW" angle, raise or lower your torso with your arms. Try extending and locking your elbows, or flattening your arms all the way till your chest rests on the bed. Explore various heights to find the angles you like—especially the one that lights up your G-spot.

🌟 **Play with him.** Hang your hair down with wild abandon, sway and gyrate your entire body to the rhythm, push back lustily on each eager thrust, gaze back and look into his eyes, reach under and caress his swaying balls, thighs and butt.

🔥 **Play with yourself.** Touch your breasts and clitoris, then reach back and massage and spank your own butt (or tell *him* to spank it). He'll go wild!

Dr. Sadie Sez: Is Super Deep Too Deep?

Some women love deep penetration. Others don't.

Guys: Never start with one long hard plunge all the way inside. Start slowly, gradually increasing your depth over several strokes. If you hear "ouch!" or "stop!" or see any signs of discomfort—STOP! A yelp from cervical pain is NOT a compliment to your lovemaking skills. You can injure her.

Ladies: If you feel any discomfort or pain, make him stop immediately. He can try a shallower stroke, or you can switch to a different position that's more comfortable. A penis buffer will prevent him from thrusting too deeply. See page 198.

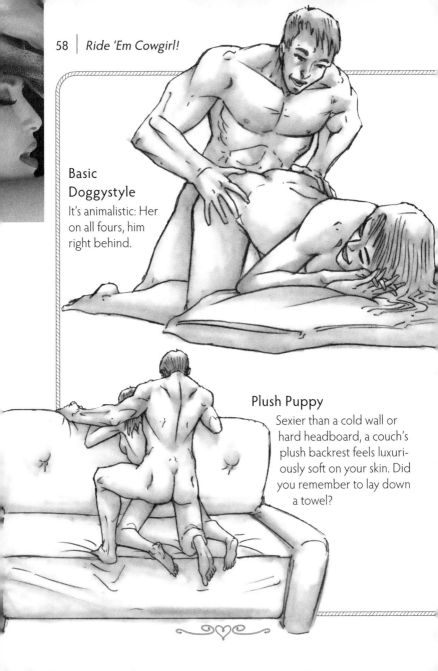

Basic Doggystyle

It's animalistic: Her on all fours, him right behind.

Plush Puppy

Sexier than a cold wall or hard headboard, a couch's plush backrest feels luxuriously soft on your skin. Did you remember to lay down a towel?

French Poodle

She turns her face for long, wet, sexy French kisses, and her clitoris stays within easy reach— for both of you.

Buried Pleasure

How deep is your love? If she lifts her knee, you'll both find out, along with soft, warm testicle-on-clitoris tapping.

Bottom's Up

Like a rest position for her, penetration is so deep, she'll get the rest of him, too. (And even some reach-under ballplay.)

Happy Crab

Stretch those quads and open the gates for uninhibited but shallower penetration and glorious G-spot pleasures.

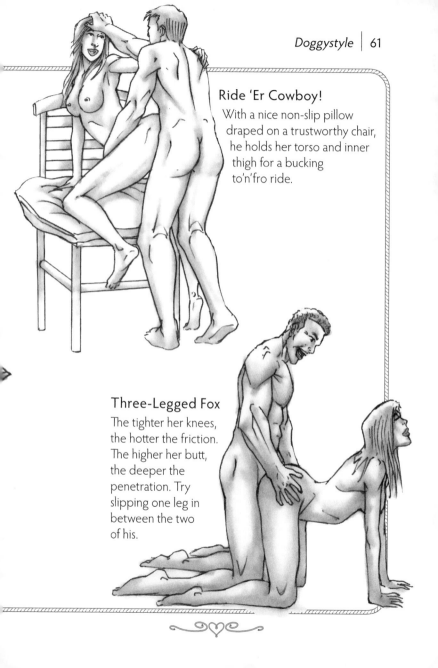

Ride 'Er Cowboy!

With a nice non-slip pillow draped on a trustworthy chair, he holds her torso and inner thigh for a bucking to'n'fro ride.

Three-Legged Fox

The tighter her knees, the hotter the friction. The higher her butt, the deeper the penetration. Try slipping one leg in between the two of his.

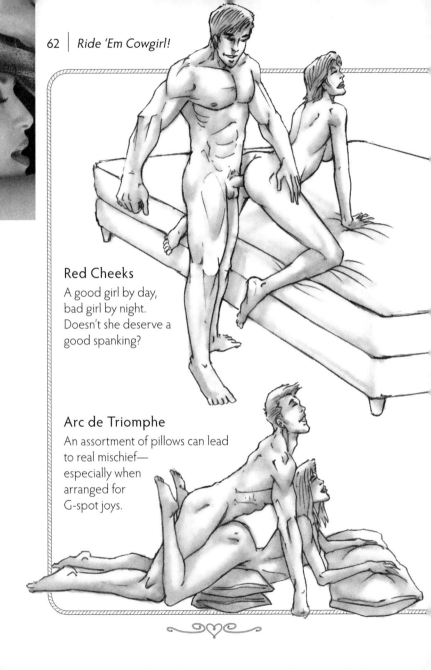

Red Cheeks

A good girl by day,
bad girl by night.
Doesn't she deserve a
good spanking?

Arc de Triomphe

An assortment of pillows can lead
to real mischief—
especially when
arranged for
G-spot joys.

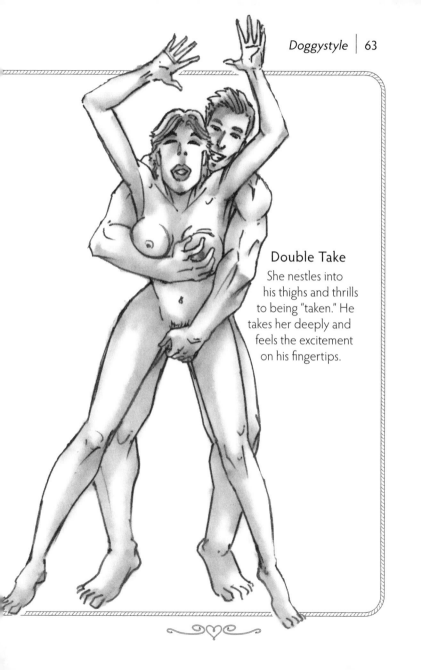

Double Take

She nestles into his thighs and thrills to being "taken." He takes her deeply and feels the excitement on his fingertips.

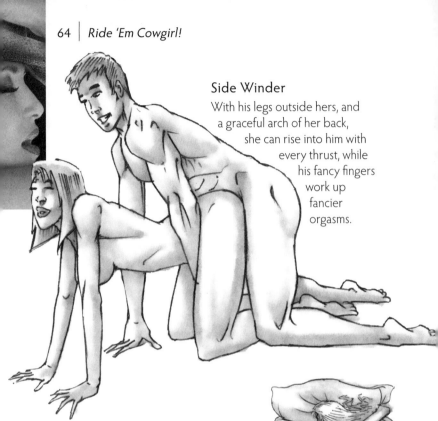

Side Winder

With his legs outside hers, and a graceful arch of her back, she can rise into him with every thrust, while his fancy fingers work up fancier orgasms.

Thumb Wrestler

A fluffy oversized pillow provides big comfort against hard momentum, especially when his slippery thumb makes a grand entrance.

7 Ride 'Em Cowgirl!

Reverse Missionary. Female Superior. Cowgirl. Whatever you call the position with the woman on top, the names often paint a vivid picture of an erotic bucking bronco ride.

But hold yer horses! Bucking is just one of the many sensual delights awaiting lovers in this position. The woman can glide sensually, rub deliciously, bounce lightly, swivel zestfully—it's entirely up to her.

That's because she's in control. SHE chooses the angle, depth, pressure and pace, guided by the primal desire to send that penis exactly where it can do the most good.

Does the excitement of the Cowgirl position come from the control? The domination? The orgasms? Or the rhythmic view of each other's naked bodies?

Yes, to all of the above.

Cowgirls Only!

Create Your Own Orgasmic Pleasures

If coming wildly during intercourse is the Holy Grail of sex, then Cowgirl will help you star as the female Indiana Jones! So glide on top and take the reins:

🌺 **Enjoy G-spot pleasures.** For increasingly delicious stimulation with every stroke, angle your body to aim the head of his penis directly at your G-spot.

🌺 **Experience clitoral joys.** For wonderful clitoral caresses with style and ease, take him all the way inside so you can rub, grind and gyrate your clitoris into the downy mound above his pubic bone.

Shape Your Pleasure
To Your Lover's Shape

With a few simple adjustments, you can ensure a near-perfect fit, whatever type of penis he's equipped with:

- **Girthier?** Try slowing the pace so his wider circumference always enters you smoothly and comfortably. Use more lube.

- **Shorter?** Tighten your PC muscles and rock or mini-pump to keep him inside you, avoiding passion-pausing "slip outs." Use less lube.

- **Lengthier?** You can glide him *juuuust* far enough inside so the joy of "hurts so good" never jolts you with just "hurts." Use a penis buffer, or try the Cover Girl position on page 73.

Shape Your Style to His Pleasure, Too

If your lover is turned on by a take-charge woman on top, here's how you can heighten pleasure even more:

- **The mount.** You're not climbing onto a mechanical bull—slink on top of him like a seductive tigress stalking her sexual prey.

🐞 **The insertion.** Before sliding him inside, grasp the head of his penis and glide it around your vulva, between your labia and around your clitoris. Spread the lubrication and feel the passion. (Careful…you may come!)

🐞 **The motion.** Start slowly, rock back and forth, gyrate in small circles, lift for sensual up'n'down stroking, and pump hard for that special *oh-oh-umph!* Your erotic moves and gyrations will stroke and caress his penis with thrilling new sensations.

🐞 **The build-up.** While he's deep inside, wrap your thumb and forefinger snugly around the base of his penis. By holding his blood in like a penis ring, you'll harden his erection. Then release your grip right as he explodes, and feel the orgasmic volcano.

🐞 **The orgasm.** As his body tenses and he nears his orgasmic point-of-no-return, match the increasing pace of his thrusting with the same speed and rhythm—and don't stop till you get his every last contraction.

🐞 **The dismount.** *Slowwwly* lift your body up and over, being careful not to knee his glowing groin. Look him in the eye and lick your lips to express your contentment. (Be sure one of you holds the base of the condom to keep it in place, too.)

You're In Charge.
Grant Him An Upgrade!

You love when he's generous in bed. Here's your chance to show that sexual generosity has no limits.

- **Be confident.** Let him feel your excitement and power rush through his entire body. Even if you act shy by day, show him what a seductress you are by night.

- **Show off.** Treat him to the ultimate eye candy: arch your back, sway slowly and gracefully, tease his chest and face with your flowing hair, offer him an erotic full-breast view, hold your labia open so he can watch his glistening penis disappear into your aroused vagina.

- **Touch him.** Explore his entire chest, neck, face, legs, arms, hips and butt with your soft sensual hands. Tease his nipples. Gently pull *his* hair. Scratch his chest. Bring your nipples to his lips. Reach around and *gently* play with his balls.

- **Touch yourself.** Here's a little secret: he's dying to watch you masturbate. Can you think of a better time to touch your clitoris—or tease yourself with a small vibrator? (He'll get off on the vibration, too!)

🐾 **Squeeze yourself.** Try gripping his penis with your vagina on each outstroke—nice and slow. It's even more heavenly if your PC muscles are in shape—see page 18.

🐾 **Shift yourself.** Why wait for him to change positions? Take charge and try some of the tempting variations in this chapter *you* want to try!

🐾 **Unmask yourself.** Cast any inhibitions to the wind and share your private, intimate orgasm-face with him—and he may share his with you.

🐾 **Tease him!** Bring him ever-so close to orgasm—then back off—again and again, till he begs for release. Who's top dog *now?*

Cowboys Only!
Don't Fall By The Waist-Side

Watching her breasts sway and her hair swirl as she takes you deep inside isn't meant to be the couch potato's ultimate wet dream. Tantalize her from down below, and feel her passions begin to flow.

Caress her head, hair and breasts. Run your hands up and down her fascinating body. Tease her nipples with fingertips you've moistened in her mouth. Kiss and suck her breasts. Tell her how hot she

looks. Hold her hips and gently help her pump and gyrate. Squeeze her butt. Touch her clitoris.

Synch up with her gyrations—and stay with them, especially when she's nearing orgasm. If she's moving slowly, stay slow. If she starts moving faster, match the pressure and speed with her in the lead. If she's running out of steam, try rolling directly into Missionary without losing your "connection."

When her orgasm is tantalizingly close, keep doing what you're doing—it's working! Stay matched to her gyrations, with perhaps an unexpected buck or grind, and even a warm, wet fingertip to her clitoris.

Basic Cowgirl

Her on top, him down below. What a perfect erotic combo.

Bucking Butterfly

She parts her lips to treat him to the best erotic eye-candy on earth, along with suddenly fuller, bouncier breasts.

Ultimate Lap Dance

By holding onto his neck and shoulders for leverage, she can rub her clitoris all over a soft, wide, inviting space (his lower tummy), while controlling his penetration depth.

Cover Girl

With her tightly wrapped legs around his, both lovers enjoy heated upper-body closeness with a snug thigh hug. If he's too long, she can easily buffer him to a more satisfying length.

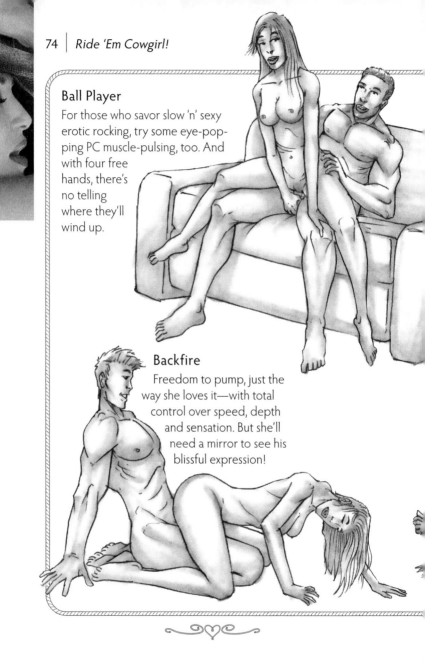

Ball Player

For those who savor slow 'n' sexy erotic rocking, try some eye-popping PC muscle-pulsing, too. And with four free hands, there's no telling where they'll wind up.

Backfire

Freedom to pump, just the way she loves it—with total control over speed, depth and sensation. But she'll need a mirror to see his blissful expression!

Ultimate Takedown

Bracing on his chest, she eases onto his erection to begin a lively bounce fest. A firm assist from his hands keeps her thighs from giving out at a key moment.

Spin Cycle

Rotate together in thrilling little circles, because regular pumping will send him popping out. What delicious eye candy for him— what tasty toe-candy for her!

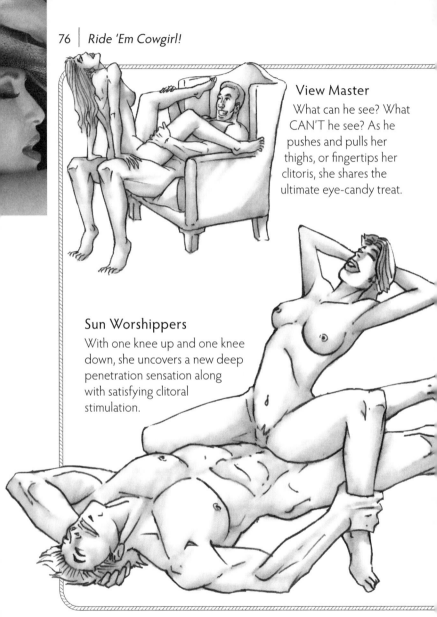

View Master

What can he see? What CAN'T he see? As he pushes and pulls her thighs, or fingertips her clitoris, she shares the ultimate eye-candy treat.

Sun Worshippers

With one knee up and one knee down, she uncovers a new deep penetration sensation along with satisfying clitoral stimulation.

Banana Split

When she slips one leg between his, and burrows his penis right into her G-spot, who do you suspect is in charge?

Bend Me, Shape Me

Don't try hard thrusting—this is only for those who love small-circle gyrating. Firm hand-assists on her hips help him keep the action in motion.

8 Spooning

If the two of you crave a position filled with wild thrusting and deep penetration, take your frenzied fingers and turn to the next chapter. Spooning ain't it.

But for those times you desire slow, sensual, romantic lovemaking, then light the candles and cuddle up close. Spooning's your ticket.

Frankly, I'd rather fork!

Spooning begins with the two of you lying comfortably on your sides, facing in the same direction. Like two matching spoons, he snuggles up close and nestles his entire body into his lover's luscious curves. For her, the excitement is enhanced by the safe, secure feeling of her beloved's intimate bear hug. For him, the thrill is sensual head-to-toe skin contact, as her soft, warm buttocks nuzzle passionately into his heat-seeking penis.

Why All The Swooning About Spooning?

Even though penetration in this position isn't super deep, and the thrusting can't be super fast, spooning brings out deeper feelings of love, intimacy and passion, along with a few unexpected delights:

 Smooth 'n' easy. Spooning is the perfect starter position for new lovers and newcomers.

♥ **Calm 'n' relaxing.** There's nothing strenuous about it—it's ideal for half-asleep morning sex.

♥ **Highly stimulating.** Her clitoris is easily reachable by his fingers —or hers!

♥ **Pleasingly shallow.** It's a great choice when you need to minimize penetration depth.

♥ **Seductively graceful.** It's comfortable for pregnant women and nice for those with body-part modesty.

♥ **Exquisitely fit.** You'll enjoy new tightness if you desire more contact and friction.

♥ **Easily transferable.** If passion mounts, roll right into Doggy-style—without losing your connection.

Spooning 101: Just Stir

Nature naturally takes over when you're spooning nude. But when she raises her upper leg and arches her lower back to extend her butt toward him, his penis can slip inside her vagina much more easily. He can then slide his body down on hers for an even more comfortable fit, creating the most pleasurable angle before the slow, gentle, excited rocking gets into full swing.

For a rush of heart-pounding pleasure, just a *slight* change of angle is all you need. Then multiply these sensations with sensual touching, and a few well-timed erotic words, and you'll reach new heights of lovemaking together.

Cowgirls Only!

She's Got Legs— And Knows How To Use 'Em

The excitement of this position all starts with your legs:

🐎 **Squeeze 'em.** For heightened pleasure, press your thighs together and hug his penis tightly by squeezing your PC muscles.

🐎 **Bend 'em.** For deeper penetration, slide your top knee up and rest your foot on your other knee—or keep raising your knee toward your shoulder, then hold it with your forearm.

Dr. Sadie Sez:
Beware Of The Unscheduled Wake-Up Call.
Spooning is the "sneaky" position—you may find him waking you up in the morning by slipping it to you. Not a bad way to greet the day, though!

🐞 **Clutch 'em.** For closer skin-to-skin rhythmic motion, swing your top leg back and over him, clutching him with your heel, and bringing him closer with every breathtaking thrust. Reach back with your hand and grip his hip to magnify the sensations.

🐞 **Cocoon 'em.** For the deepest penetration, raise both your knees to your chest, as he inches his body down for the most sensual angle of all.

Cowboys Only!
Don't Fall Behind

Since this is one of the most romantic positions of all, why not add to the feeling with a few sensual touches of your own:

💋 **Kiss her.** Bring your lips to her neck to tease her with angel kisses, and feel her shudder with delight. When you sense she's close to climax, bite her neck lightly.

- 👤 **Touch her.** Hold her head in your hands. Play with her hair. Massage her neck. Run your fingers over her lips. Caress her breasts. Tease her nipples. Give her goosebumps with all your skin-to-skin contact.

- 👤 **Hug her.** Bring her entire body close to yours. When she lifts her leg, help her support it in the most comfortable position.

- 👤 **Tease her.** Reach around and gently fingertip her clitoris to bring her to a glorious orgasm or two.

Sporking

From romantic to ravaging, this uninhibited spooning position opens her for full thrusting and hot clitoral stimulation by pinning her thigh open with his arm.

Basic Spooning

Like two spoons in a drawer… only a LOT more stimulating.

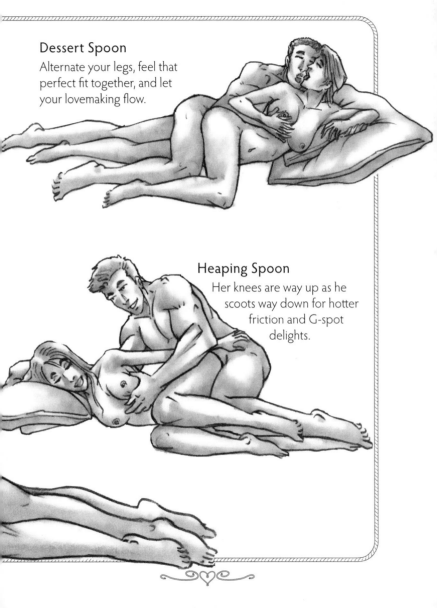

Dessert Spoon

Alternate your legs, feel that perfect fit together, and let your lovemaking flow.

Heaping Spoon

Her knees are way up as he scoots way down for hotter friction and G-spot delights.

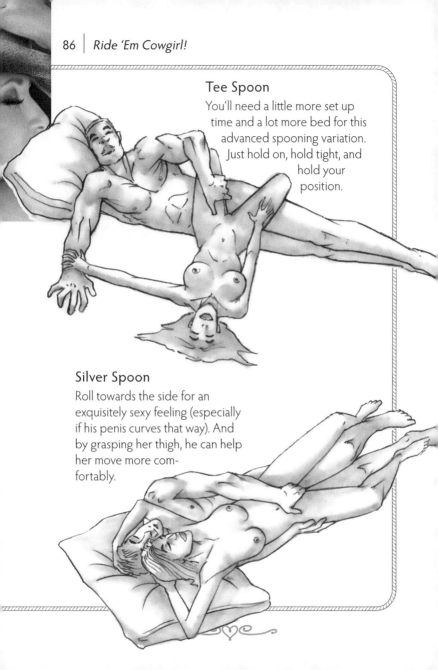

Tee Spoon

You'll need a little more set up time and a lot more bed for this advanced spooning variation. Just hold on, hold tight, and hold your position.

Silver Spoon

Roll towards the side for an exquisitely sexy feeling (especially if his penis curves that way). And by grasping her thigh, he can help her move more comfortably.

9 Clitilicious

Well, which is it? Kli-TOR-iss…or KLIT-uh-riss?

It's both. But more important, why is it so easily left out of love-making?

In one of those great unexplained mysteries of the universe, nearly every act of intercourse brings the clitoris *ever-so-close* to the hot delicious friction a woman needs to come.

Close. But no cookie.

Through no fault of womankind, in nearly every position women love, the clitoris is left out of the action to watch the penis plunge merrily towards its own happy ending.

Come on, let's shoot for equal rights with lubrication and orgasms for all!

What (And Where) Is The Clitoris Anyhow?

The clitoris is the *only* human organ dedicated 100 percent to bringing heart-pounding, toe-curling, breathtaking orgasmic pleasure to women. That's quite remarkable for an organ about the size of a small pea.

Nestled into the top of the vulva where both sets of labia come together, the clitoris is hidden slightly from view in its own cozy alcove under the clitoral hood. When lovingly aroused, the clitoris can double in size, emerge gloriously, and glow rosy red as orgasm nears.

But there's more to the clitoris than meets the tongue. New research shows its *real* size may actually be closer to that of an entire penis! From just beneath its visible pea-shaped head, the two clitoral legs (*crura*) hug the entire length of the vaginal canal. This may well trigger clitoral stimulation from deep penetration. But the *real* heart-pounding pleasure comes from that tiny visible clitoral head, just aching to be touched.

Two Sensitive Heads— One Super Craving

As opposite as the sexes often seem, women and men share one important sexual similarity—the workings of their sexual pleasure centers. Here's why:

♥ The clitoris is micro-clustered with millions of the same type of erotic nerve endings found in the head of the penis.

♥ Men become erect during arousal—and so do women! As the clitoris swells with blood, it swells in size. Next time, feel it grow from small and subtle to round and firm as foreplay heats up.

♥ There's rarely an orgasm without direct stimulation to the head of the penis. Likewise, there's rarely an orgasm if you neglect the clitoris.

♥ The clitoris and the penis respond best when slippery-wet. Did you remember to pick up a good sex lube?

By understanding these similarities, it's easy to see why it's vital to stimulate the tiny but powerful clitoris *directly*, especially during intercourse.

Guys...*please read that last sentence again!*

20 Ways To Supercharge Intercourse

Between the two of you, you'll find 20 warm, soft, active little clitoral stimulators that you'll never misplace, need no batteries, and can lift the woman to the highest orgasmic peaks on earth.

They're your fingertips—just add sex lube!

The fingertip secret is to touch the clitoris with slow, gentle caressing motions, matching the pressure and pace to the level of her arousal. Just be sure there's lots of lubrication, start slow and soft, and you can't go wrong.

Whoever is doing the arousing, vary your fingertip motions till you find a pattern that works: up'n'down, side-to-side, round'n'round, or even figure eights. For a real treat, try these motions with the tip of the penis.

Cowboys Only!

Coming During Intercourse (Not You...*Her!*)

When a woman finally catches her breath after her first deep-penetration orgasm, she may lovingly whisper those magical ego-boosting words, "No one's ever done *THAT* to me before!" Here's how to do *THAT*:

- ☙ **Grind.** When you're deep inside, gently press your soft pubic mound into her clitoris and grind till you discover the moves that set her off.

- ☙ **Fingerplay.** Reach over, under or around and gently fingertip her clitoris in harmony with your thrusting.

- **Accessorize.** Surprise her with a sensual gift: a small bullet vibrator to tantalize her clitoris during lovemaking.

- **Ask:** "How does *this* feel?" or "Do you want it faster?" Let her guide you. Then do what she says!

- **Preheat.** Use your talented tongue or frisky fingertips to bring her within moments of a huge orgasm. NOW—quickly slide your penis inside and finish her off by gyrating in small circles against her clitoris.

The Mystery Of The Missionary Orgasm Revealed!

Did you know that one little adjustment to your Missionary technique can unleash a torrent of wild penetration orgasms in your lover? Here's how:

Place a small pillow under her hips, and ease your lubricated penis deep inside her. Now slide your entire body high-up on hers, so you are pelvis-to-pelvis. As you stroke down and in, the base of your penis will directly stimulate her clitoris, then grind your pubic mound into her in little circles. Try visualizing her clitoris as you press on it, and resist the temptation to lift off and thrust in and out. Just keep your penis tucked snugly inside her, and sway in small circles to find the rhythm she needs. You'll know it's starting to work when you feel her holding you tighter while she begs you to speed up.

Dr. Sadie Sez:
Ladies! Missionary Orgasms! For Real!

When your guy rides up on you in Missionary, and grinds deliciously into your clitoris, move your hips in harmony with him to help him find your spot. Then let him know with a simple, *"Ohhh, just like THAT!"* Wrap your legs around him, pull him tighter, and focus on your rising passion. If you want it faster, tell him. And when you reach that point-of-no-return, whisper (or shout!) what's about to happen…

Cushion Pushin'

Holding his neck (or back of the couch) for balance, she can pleasure-rub or power-thrust—or both!

Wrap Party

She hugs his body tight, he pulls her close, and both press and grind in harmony.

Wishboner

She arches her back to angle her hips down, he arches his back to offer his pubic region. Both grind to a fantastic finish.

Snug Smuggler

Snug for her, with exquisite pressure on her clitoris, and snug for him, with the unique sensation of snuggly hugged balls.

High Rider

He rides high, pressing her clitoris with each stroke. She grabs his hips and stimulates powerful orgasms.

Tumbleweed

Tightly intertwined bodies offer direct clitoral contact as he rocks, gyrates and looks deep into her eyes.

Stargazer

Fun to try, easy to slip out. But if you're both built for this position, her clitoris is always within fingertip reach.

10 The G-spot

Every woman on earth is graced with a G-spot—a powerful epicenter of deep, satisfying, body-pulsing orgasms—yet none can experience its profound pleasures without the secret of its magic touch.

Hello, guys…are you listening?

What And Where Is The G-spot?

The G-spot is a small, ridged, oval-ish area of spongy tissue that's 2-to-3 inches inside the vagina, on its upper wall, just behind the pubic hairline.

G-spot epicenter

The right touch can be pleasureful beyond belief, but the G-spot also serves an important biological purpose. During sexual excitement, it swells with blood to cushion the urethral cord it surrounds, protecting the woman's delicate urinary passageway from her lover's rapid-fire pleasure-pounding.

The G-spot is easier to locate than you might imagine. Slide a lubricated finger or two inside the vagina, along the upper wall, with fingertips facing up so you can curve your fingers toward the belly. At 2-to-3 inches inside, when the vagina's sensual softness turns to sensational ridgy-ness—*eureka*—you've found it!

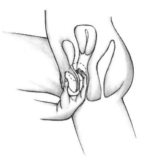

To the touch, the G-spot feels a little bulgy, about the area of a quarter, with ridges that feel much like those along the roof of your mouth (run the tip of your tongue up top now for a free demo). If you have trouble finding it, try exploring after some heated foreplay, when it swells from stimulation and excitement.

Mastering The G-Spot Magic Touch

Touching the G-spot with the same gentle caressing that excites the clitoris probably won't create the erotic heat you seek. Here's why.

While the clitoris is super-packed with millions of touch-sensitive pleasure receptors, the G-spot is not. However, the G-spot

does respond in a big way to a different type of erotic stimulation: pressure.

If you're ready to experience explosive G-spot orgasms, just stroke it firmly and directly with a finger, a G-spot sextoy, and of course, the head of a heat-seeking penis.

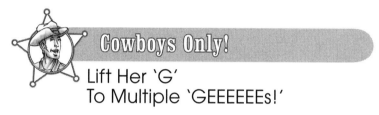

Cowboys Only!
Lift Her 'G' To Multiple 'GEEEEEEs!'

No cold-starts allowed! First, turn her on with your most stimulating foreplay—and preferably a clitoral orgasm or two. Now she'll be fully pre-heated, and her G-spot will be bigger and easier to find.

Touch your fingertip directly to her G-spot, and gently bend and unbend your knuckle as if to gesture "come here" (you *are*, actually!). Gradually increase the pressure of your touch. Try new rhythms. Stroke in small circles. Tap rapidly. Add in a second finger. You get the idea….

If your lover doesn't seem to be feeling the excitement yet, try asking, "How does *that* feel?" and let her guide you. Once you find her desired pleasure style, you'll feel her G-spot grow larger and firmer as her entire body responds with excitement.

For a delicious crescendo, double her pleasure by touching your finger, tongue or a vibrator to her clitoris for simultaneous stimulation that can set her off like a live volcano. (Most women *need* this double-touch to experience a G-spot orgasm.) After she climaxes in a heart-racing frenzy, everything will then feel overly sensitive to her, and she may need more time before starting up again. Just go softly and slowly.

Yet Another G-spot Magic Touch

Did you know you can stimulate her G-spot from *outside* her body, too? Here's how: While your fingers are pleasuring her G-spot inside her vagina, place the fingers of your other hand on her lower abdomen. Now gently press all your fingertips together from both hands, and squeeze her G-spot in the middle. *Whoa yeah!*

Dr. Sadie Sez:
Look For The Curved Excitement Tip.

Just like the fingers you curl upward to pleasure her G-spot (be sure to trim and file your nails), G-spot toys all come with a similarly curved tip to angle the pressure right where she loves it. Try a G-spot vibrator together with your oral love, and send her to orgasm nirvana.

The G-spot Position Decision

When your penis brings her to frenzied G-spot orgasms, she knows she's with a first-class lover. Come claim your upgrade:

- **Visualize.** Upon penetration, picture the location of her G-spot in your mind, then aim the head of your penis directly into it. Since it's only 2-to-3 inches inside, you'll also have to keep resisting the urge to go deep.

- **Lead.** In most positions, *you're* in control, so it's up to you to create the angle, speed, pressure and depth that'll set her off.

- **Ask.** It's okay to ask if you've found her spot with a simple, "How's that?" You'll also find out which stroking patterns and rhythms she likes. Then, once you're spot-on, the two of you can gyrate in perfect synch.

- **Balance.** For greater stability and control, grasp her hips or butt cheeks firmly. You'll also give her greater leverage to grind back on you.

- **Thumbs Up.** Once you've found her rhythm, gently press your thumb onto her sensitive anus. Even the *slightest* pressure along with G-spot stimulation will send her over the pleasure edge.

Dr. Sadie Sez: Knock, Knock. . . Banana Who?
Were you born with that rarest of gifts, the curved penis? Congratulations—you're an instant winner (and so is your lover)! You can target her G-spot without trying, especially in Missionary. For a satisfied smile, just send in your natural banana. Orange you glad you did?

🂠 **Double Down.** Now skyrocket her arousal with some heavenly clitoral stimulation—and propel her into uncharted orgasmic orbits.

Cowgirls Only!
Come Meet Your G-spot

How sensational is G-spot pleasure, really? Can it truly be as orgasmically thrilling as many claim? Hop on and find out:

🂠 **The sensation.** At first, the "feel" of G-spot pressure may take some getting used to. When touched, you may sense a slight burning (but in a good way), a light tickle, discomfort, nothing at all, or, of course, pleasure.

🂠 **The urge.** It's also normal to feel like you have to pee when pressure is applied to your G-spot (you *are* pressing on the urethra). Relax—you won't pee—it's a feeling that'll turn to

pure pleasure very soon. For greater comfort, empty your bladder beforehand.

The assist. When your lover finally finds your G-spot, you'll know. So let *him* know! A simple, "Oh yeah, right there!" or "Back up, *YESSSS!*" oughta do it.

The retry. Discomfort? Pain? Then say so! Is he pushing too hard or at a wrong angle? Tell him to lighten up or vary his approach. Still uncomfortable? Have him withdraw and start over a few moments later—often that helps a lot.

The takeover. Is he not finding your groove? Then take control. Try Cowgirl, angling yourself for a G-spot jackpot. Or try Dog-gystyle, tilt and tuck your pelvis back into him till you find your perfect orgasmic fit.

The prize. Once he's found your spot, build to your orgasm by squeezing and holding your PC muscles the entire time

Dr. Sadie Sez: Master Your OWN G-spot!

Who says you need a partner to locate and pleasure your G-spot? Why not treat yourself to a G-spot toy, designed to seek out and satisfy. You can find them in different styles and colors online, or at a sextoy store. Go ahead and splurge. You deserve it!

he's stroking you. Add in clitoral stimulation with a finger-tip or vibrator, focusing only on the pleasure, and feel your passions rise.

The Surprise Of The Liquid Orgasm

As it turns out, men aren't the only humans blessed with the ability to ejaculate.

Women, too, can spout naturally during orgasm, especially a powerful G-spot orgasm.

If you experience "female ejaculations," they're nothing to be embarrassed about. In fact, they're something to be proud of. Your lover may be very turned-on by your liquid orgasms, too.

Contrary to what many people think, this liquid is *not* urine. It comes from specialized glands that surround the urethra—and is surprisingly similar to the fluid produced by the male prostate. Here's what to expect: at the moment of liquid orgasm, the woman's ejaculate either dribbles slowly or spurts wildly out of the urethra. Its color may be clear or milky, its texture is thin like water, and it may taste slightly sweet, a bit tart, or even have no taste at all. In fact, the major difference between male and female ejaculate is that hers has no sperm.

A woman's liquid orgasm feels good too, like adding an indescribable heated *oomph* to an already powerful climax. Whether you're graced with the ability to create liquid orgasms, or you begin ejaculating when you experiment with G-spot orgasms, don't be shy—let it fly! And save yourselves the clean-up by spreading out a large towel before the waterworks begin!

World's Top G-spot Positions

G Marks The Spot

Both grind in tiny circles, he resists the in'n'out temptation, and she keeps his penis pressed into her G-spot. Want more gyrating power? She leans forward and hugs his neck.

Doggystyle G

Up goes her butt and down goes her chest while he rides her high. A few well-placed pillows under her hips and you're off to the races!

Bull's-eye

For precise aim and a snug fit, his legs go outside hers. She holds perfectly still till he presses into her G-spot, then both gyrate together as her fingers find her clitoris.

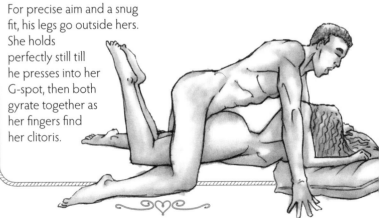

G-spa

For a total stimulation package of neck nibbling, breast caressing, clitoral fingertipping and G-spot gyration, come visit the G-spa.

Lady Godiva

Hold still, mister! She's ready to rock out right on her own G-spot. As she's nearing a lusty finish, he grasps her hips and sends her gyrations into overdrive.

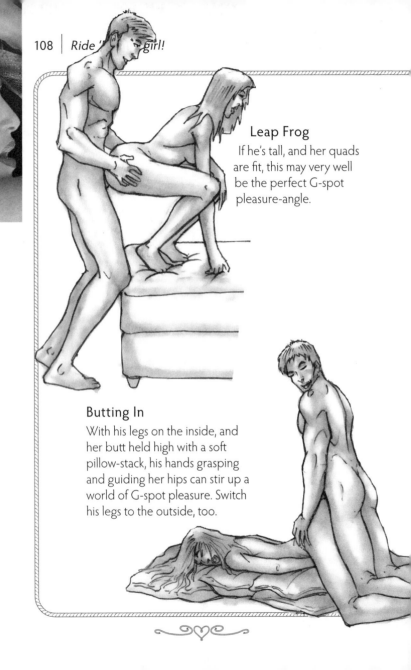

Leap Frog

If he's tall, and her quads are fit, this may very well be the perfect G-spot pleasure-angle.

Butting In

With his legs on the inside, and her butt held high with a soft pillow-stack, his hands grasping and guiding her hips can stir up a world of G-spot pleasure. Switch his legs to the outside, too.

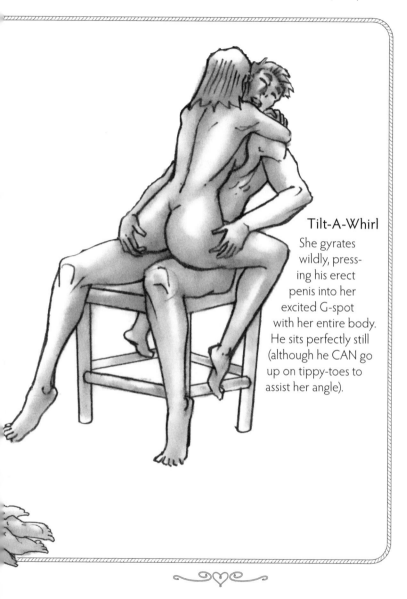

Tilt-A-Whirl

She gyrates wildly, pressing his erect penis into her excited G-spot with her entire body. He sits perfectly still (although he CAN go up on tippy-toes to assist her angle).

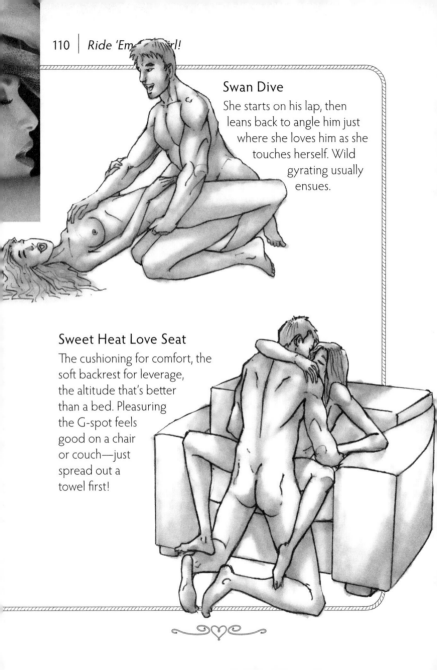

Swan Dive

She starts on his lap, then leans back to angle him just where she loves him as she touches herself. Wild gyrating usually ensues.

Sweet Heat Love Seat

The cushioning for comfort, the soft backrest for leverage, the altitude that's better than a bed. Pleasuring the G-spot feels good on a chair or couch—just spread out a towel first!

11 Backdoor Boogaloo

Yup, it's exactly what you think it is. Anal sex.

If those two little words send a shiver down your spine (and not the thrilling kind), you might want to read the next paragraph twice.

When you discover the *safe, savvy way* to enjoy anal sex, you can awaken a deep romantic connection with your lover, as well as eye-popping, spine-tingling, full-body orgasms beyond your wildest imagination.

BACK DOOR
DO NOT
ENTER!

Yet, anal sex *is* an acquired taste. Few women enjoy it the first time, mostly due to poor preparation and heat-of-the-moment partner-pressure. This often results in unnecessary discomfort and pain that makes one wonder why anyone would ever do it, let alone *enjoy* it.

But if you start off with good information, preparation and communication, anal sex can become one of life's most deeply erotic adventures—one that many more heterosexual couples privately rave about today more than ever before.

"Yes, but…"

Hesitant? Curious? Eager? Then please read on. Talk about it with your lover. See if it sets your hearts racing. And you too may soon switch your position to—"Yes, butt!"

Why The Fascination With Anal?

As you surely know, most hetero guys are ready, willing and thwarted by that well-worn feminine phrase: "Not in *this* lifetime."

So why *would* you try anal sex in this lifetime? The reason has as much to do with tasting the forbidden fruit as it does with a delightful quirk of feminine anatomy: the G-spot can actually receive incredible stimulation through anal sex—and in some cases—even more than through vaginal intercourse.

It gets better: As he lovingly fingertips the clitoris, and his slippery-hot penis tantalizes the rich, sensitive nerve endings in her anus, all while he's excitedly stimulating her G-spot, a woman may experience the most astounding whole-body orgasms she's ever felt—indescribable pulsations of passion that can't be achieved any other way.

At least in this lifetime.

The 4 Guidelines For Enjoying Anal Sex

Whether you're an anal sex virgin, or trying to overcome any memories of past discomforts, start with these four easy guidelines to ensure your pleasure, comfort and safety:

♥ **Talk.** Anal sex is not a spur-of-the-moment act. It takes planning, provisions and discussion (an intimate conversation you're likely to find *very* arousing!). You must also communicate with each other throughout the entire experience. It's a shared pleasure that requires trust, confidence and responsibility.

♥ **Relax.** The anus stays tight for a good reason, and learning to relax the sphincter muscles and get accustomed to fingers, sex-toys or a penis takes time. Initially, you *may* feel a little discomfort before you feel pleasure, and while the level is different for everyone, it should NEVER be painful. Follow the advice in this chapter and you'll ease into enjoyment much more quickly.

♥ **Practice.** Most of the women who overcame reluctance and now enjoy anal sex say it took three or four tries to get it right. Be patient. Be positive. Be proactive. And follow these guidelines. Once you learn what you like, anal sex gets more comfortable each time.

♥ **Be safe.** Even if you are in a totally monogamous relationship, anal sex can spread bacteria that can lead to infections. You MUST follow all precautions below.

> **SAFER SEX PRECAUTION.** *Anal sex without a condom puts you at risk of sexually transmitted infections and diseases. Play it safe. Read AND PRACTICE all the safer sex tips in this chapter and in the Appendix at the end of this book.*

Precautions & Preparations For Anal Sex

Anal sex is more pleasurable when your physical and mental safeguards are in place. Practice these safeguards every time:

♥ **Use latex barriers.** Roll a spermicide-free latex condom over the penis. Wear latex gloves or single finger covers (*finger cots*) if inserting fingers. Place a latex dam or sheet of plastic wrap between any tongue-to-anus stimulation (*analingus* or "rimming")—or cut a fresh latex condom lengthwise and lay it flat. Never invert or reuse any latex barriers—always toss them out.

♥ **Wash up.** If it will come in contact with the anus, pre-wash it in hot water with antibacterial soap. This includes fingers, sextoys and yourselves. File down and smooth out all rough edges on sextoys and fingernails, too.

♥ **Single dip only.** Once you've committed to the back door— the vagina and mouth are off limits till after the penis and hands are thoroughly washed, or you'll risk introducing germs that can lead to infection.

♥ **Get slippery.** Unlike the vagina, the rectum is delicate and dry, with no natural lubrication to glide the penis inside. You MUST squeeze on the lube—in large, generous amounts! And don't even *think* about using saliva.

♥ **Choose proper sextoys.** Use sextoys made specifically for anal play. Never slide anything into the anus that does not have a flared base or extra-long handle to grip, otherwise it can get sucked inside. Make sure you've filed smooth any rough plastic seams. And roll a fresh condom over your sextoys.

A Word About...*Er*...Poop!

You were wondering, right? Well relax, it's no big deal.

To clear your mind, as well as your rectum, just go to the bathroom beforehand. When you feel empty, or if you've had a bowel

movement within the previous few hours, you should be fine. Your five-inch rectum normally stays clear until you get "the signal" that it's time to go again. If you get that feeling *once he's inside*, that's normal, but it's most likely *him*. Enjoy!

Will you need an enema beforehand? Nope—but feel free. Should you wash down there in advance? Yes—lather up well. Will any poop come out on whatever you insert? Perhaps—just clean it up with some disposable wipes or a warm, wet, dark-colored washcloth (no need to "see" any mess). Might there be farting? Probably—you're pushing air up there. It's funny—so just laugh!

Cowgirls Only!
Insider Tips For Smoother Anal

When you've decided to explore the joys of anal sex, and after you've talked with your lover about safety, lubrication and being patient, here are a few ways to ease into the pleasure:

- ♣ **Heat up.** The best primer for anal sex—is sex itself. Enjoy a round or two of oral orgasms or vaginal intercourse to get the blood flowing to all the right places. Try using a small butt plug during Doggystyle, or let his lubed finger get things started.

- 🧘 **Open up.** Since the anus is naturally tight, the secret to accepting his lubricated penis is to lightly push outward with your anal muscles, while he's gently inserting.

- 🧘 **Speak up.** Don't be shy. Say what you're thinking so he'll know he's being a great lover. Try "slower" or "not so deep" or *"ouch!"* or *"YESSS!" Note:* some guys don't believe "stop" really means "STOP." It's better to create a "safe word"—a secret word you both agree *in advance* will really mean "STOP!" (e.g. "Pancake!")

- 🧘 **Ease up.** Relax. Breathe deeply. Don't clench or stiffen. This is mind over body—and you're in control, because pleasure is your goal.

- 🧘 **Loosen up.** While drugs and hard liquor can easily lead to sloppy preparation and poor decision-making, a glass of wine might be just the ticket to relaxing and getting into the zone.

- 🧘 **Bottoms up.** Although you may come to love anal sex, you're not obligated to do it often. Think of it more as a special, naughty erotic treat!

Cowboys Only!

How To Be Her Anal Hero

After you've talked it over, and agreed to try it, this isn't your cue to barge right in. It IS your cue to show her you're a world-class lover (or plan on kissing her butt goodbye!).

- **Preheat.** She needs you to begin slowly and lovingly to start her hot blood rushing to the scene. Best way? Hot foreplay with an orgasm or two. You know you're doing it right if she *never* tells you to slow down.

- **Touch.** Show her you've got talented, confident hands by using them to seduce her lower back, inner thighs and butt cheeks. Kiss her all over. Take your time.

- **Tongue.** Whip her into a frenzy by licking and kissing her vagina, clitoris, then her ultra-sensitive anus. Flick gently before you tease the tip in and out.

- **Nestle.** Gently slide a well-lubricated finger into her anus, but only to the first knuckle. Now hold it still. Feel her sphincter involuntarily pulsating around your digit. Now wiggle, just a little, and relax her muscles even more.

- **Excite.** Slide in your finger a little further to the second knuckle, but resist stroking in'n'out. Hold still, and see if you feel her

> **Dr. Sadie Sez: For A Big Rush, Just Go Slow.**
> Even though you've talked it over, she may not be ready for anal sex. Instead, try treating her to other stimulating anal pleasures. Fingertip just the outside of her anus. Tease her with the tip of your tongue. If she's okay with it, gently insert a lubed finger or a small butt plug. If you gradually increase stimulation, perhaps someday she'll be penis-ready. Or just give her this book to read on her own.

loosening up. Whisper, "I'm holding my finger still…just relax." When you feel her relax, tell her you're going to gently wiggle your finger again. Then do it.

- **Double Excite.** What's your free hand up to? What's your mouth doing? Reach around or dive down and excite her clitoris. You're doing everything right if she's now completely, totally, passionately turned on.

The Art Of Anal Penetration

This is the moment of truth, where all your skills as a lover come into play. You're both fully lubed, she's completely preheated, and you're sheathed in a condom, right?

- **Missile guidance.** With your hand, ease the tip of your well-lubed penis inside her well-lubed anus. Use gentle slow

pressure—don't force! If she's nervous, it may take time till her involuntary sphincter muscles relax. Be sure to stimulate her clitoris simultaneously—it feels good, relaxes the muscles, and offsets any discomfort with pure pleasure.

🐞 **Align by design.** Stay on a smooth path to entry, adjusting and angling yourself to match her natural angle. After she takes in the first few inches of your penis, *stay motionless for awhile* and feel her pulsating anus dancing around you. Keep touching her clitoris.

🐞 **Go slowly.** Begin *slow, shallow* thrusting—it's too soon to go deep, especially if she's new at this. Pay attention to what feels good to her, and keep stimulating her clitoris.

🐞 **Stop when she says, "STOP!"** Immediately. And never pull out suddenly. Ask what's wrong. If she feels anything more than slight discomfort, adjust your angle, slow your pace, don't go so deep, add more lube, or all of the above.

🐞 **Glide into pleasure.** Stay slow and shallow to ease any discomfort. Watch her hips move. See your penis penetrate. Find your stride. Feel her pleasure. But pace yourself—it's tighter than a vagina—and you may be done before she comes! (You're still stimulating her clitoris, right?)

The Art Of Anal Loving

Giving anal sex feels so good, it's easy to get lost in your own pleasure and forget hers. But staying focused on her pleasure can set off the strongest total-body orgasms she's ever felt. Here's how to take full credit for it:

- **Reach around.** Most women need clitoral stimulation to orgasm—so you must keep caressing her clitoris while you're inside her. It can make the difference between doing it right, or never doing it again.

- **Take aim.** Angle your penis to try and stroke her G-spot with every thrust. But if you're a newcomer, just focus on basic pleasure techniques and work up to it.

- **Get buzzed.** Have a small vibrator on hand for one of you to press gently into her clitoris. You should feel the vibes coming through her skin, too!

- **Dismount gracefully.** Always remove your penis slowly, and remember to grasp the base of the condom and slide it out together with your penis. Don't spill or splash its contents. Have a clean towel or disposable wipes handy to clear away any excess.

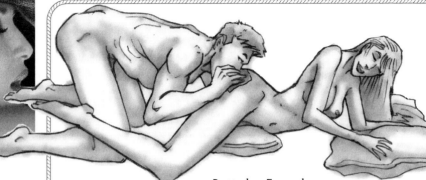

Buttplay Foreplay

Seduce. Finesse. Tease. Tantalize.
But never lunge or plunge.

Backdoor Missionary

Best for newcomers. Comfortable. Familiar. Connected.
You can see and share signs of pleasure or uncertainty while you kiss passionately. Pillows help with support.

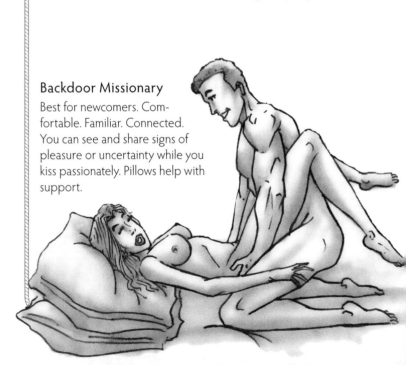

Full Spoon

This comfortable, intimate starter position is especially good if there's a big size difference between you.

Quarterback Sneak

Adjust her height and ensure her comfort with pillows—and prop the chair against bed or sofa to prevent sudden tip-overs.

Plunge Diver

She's in charge now, setting depth, stroking and speed to whatever's comfortable for her. A sensual face-to-face intimacy bonus, too.

Easy Rider

Another good position where she's in full command, especially when she lusts for reverse cowgirl pleasures.

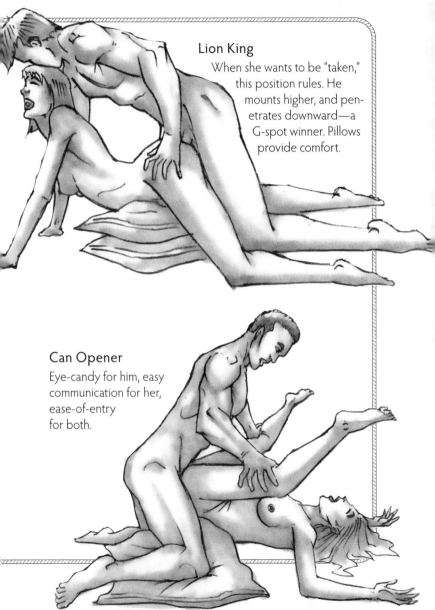

Lion King

When she wants to be "taken," this position rules. He mounts higher, and penetrates downward—a G-spot winner. Pillows provide comfort.

Can Opener

Eye-candy for him, easy communication for her, ease-of-entry for both.

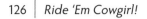

Hot Heinie

Nice starter position, with her controlling the angle and depth of penetration, while her lips and clitoris are always within his easy reach.

Rump Roast

She extends her legs fully, and takes him in deeply while laying there comfortably.

12 The HE-Spot

ttention Cowgirls: What if you discovered a whole new way to give your guy the hottest, wildest, most intense orgasms of his life? Might this erotic breakthrough open the door to deeper intimacy, a healthier relationship and a brand new Ferrari?

Would you settle for two out of three?

While there's no question that your new powers would have him kissing the ground you walk on, you may not be prepared for his initial response to your seductive suggestion: "No thanks."

Huh?

127

That's right. Your explosive orgasmic temptation comes with a *but*—all this pleasure takes place within his *butt!*

Say Hello To The HE-spot

All women have a G-spot. And all guys have their own orgasm spot, too. It's called a prostate.

Located at the intersection of the urinary and reproductive tracts, just behind the base of the penis, at about one to three inches inside, this walnut-sized gland's primary purpose is to produce and store much of the milky fluid that gives sperm its pulsing liquid ride out of his body.

This gland has a pleasure purpose, too. If a woman caresses her lover's prostate directly with her fingertip, she can drive him insane with delight—but only if that loving finger is permitted to reach knuckle-deep inside his anus—an act that's been known to turn even the most macho man into a bowlful of quivering jelly.

Right now, hold up your index finger where you can examine it closely. Does it really look all that scary?

Cowboys Only!
You Shall Overcome

Question: Isn't buttplay gay?
Answer: It's about as gay as a penis in a vagina!

Here's the honest truth: When buttplay is enjoyed by a woman with a man, that's as hetero as it gets. *It's not a sexual preference— it's a sexual pleasure.*

Today, as more women take up the reins of erotic play, anal stimulation has come into the sexual mainstream, with increasing numbers of heterosexual couples trying *and enjoying it* in the privacy of their own homes. Why? One reason might play out something like this:

He: "Honey, can we, *y'know*, perhaps, *uhhh*, try some anal sex tonight?"
She: "Sure dear. You first!"

If turnabout is fair play, that could explain why sales of prostate stimulators and other buttplay toys among hetero couples are, forgive the pun, surging. Find out more in chapter 18.

So how about you, cowboy? Are *you* ready to experience orgasms beyond your wildest imagination?

Cowgirls Only!

Ease Up A Butt.
Then Take Charge!

Sure, the first time touching his HE-spot can be awkward for you, too. *Relax.* You'll find everything here to start you off on the right, *er,* finger!

- 🎎 **Talk up.** Start by reading this chapter together, discussing and even laughing about it. Rather than focusing on the process, envision the results: off-the-Richter-scale orgasms and a higher level of intimacy and sexual maturity. If he's still unwilling, that's okay—don't twist his arm. He may come around eventually.

- 🎎 **Study up.** If there's interest, try watching a sensual massage DVD together to see how the stars' skilled hands caress the butt and inner thighs. Or slip in an erotic DVD that features a bit of anal play for even more probing ideas.

- 🎎 **Clean up.** Shortly before your big romantic rendezvous, suggest he go to the bathroom to empty his bladder and bowel—or enjoy a warm enema—all followed by a hot shower. Better

yet, jump in and soap him up yourself to be sure he hasn't missed any essential spots.

🦋 **Shave up.** Is he a bit too "furry" down there? Create yet another erotic adventure and shave his butt. His skin will become more sensitized, and even more welcoming for a gentle, probing tongue.

Precautions & Preparations For HE-spot Play

🦋 **Wash. Wash. Wash.** Rule of thumb: If it will come in contact with the anus, pre-wash it in hot water with antibacterial soap. This includes hands, sextoys and yourselves. Be sure to file down and smooth out any rough edges on sextoys, too.

🦋 **Smooth. Smooth. Smooth.** File all your nails till they're perfectly smooth, and remove all rings from your fingers. If your nails are long, wear latex gloves with a ball of cotton in each of the tips.

🦋 **Lube. Lube. Lube.** Slather on plenty of sex lubricant, because his anus is naturally dry and delicate, and can easily tear from unlubricated friction. Use generous amounts of sex lube *every time* you engage in anal play—and *never substitute it with quick-drying saliva.*

🐾 **Slow. Slow. Slow.** Always enter the anus *slowwwly*. Always exit the anus *slowwwly*. Never slide anything into the anus that does not have a flared base or extra-long handle to grip, or it can get sucked inside.

🐾 **Cover. Cover. Cover.** To protect against unwanted bacteria-transfer, use a latex dam during tongue play—a thin sheet you place between the tongue and anus, which transfers only the erotic sensations. Or use a sheet of plastic wrap from the kitchen. For finger play, wear a latex glove or a single finger cover (finger cot). And unroll a fresh condom over any sextoy to keep it bacteria-free. Of course, you'll also remember to lube up, right?

> **PRECAUTIONS.** *Anal play without a condom puts you at risk of sexually transmitted diseases and infections. Anal play without lube risks tearing the delicate lining in the rectum. HE-spot massage is not recommended during any prostate disorder. Please read AND PRACTICE all the safer sex tips in this chapter and in the Appendix at the end of this book.*

Going In For The Thrill

Your first time can be very arousing—like you're both virgins again. Go slowly, find the positions you like, feel the excitement build, and enjoy all the naughty new sensations.

🐾 **Warm up.** Massage his inner thighs and inner butt cheeks, then try some oral love, swirling your hot tongue from his penis, closer and closer to your target. At the right moment, flick the tip of your tongue lightly on his tightly puckered anus You'll not only send tingles throughout his body, you'll swell his HE-spot so it's easier to find and primed for your sensual touch.

🐾 **Lube up.** Slather the sex lube on everything that will enter him. Try a nicely flavored lube if one of those objects will be your tongue. Now gently press your slippery fingertip onto his pulsing anus as your hot mouth once again finds his throbbing penis.

🐾 **Butt in.** Slowly, sensually, insert your fully lubed index finger (or middle finger), inching it along the upper wall toward the base of his penis. Feel his rectum naturally curve toward the front of his body, along with the natural curve of your finger.

🐾 **Play around.** Now that he's all slippery-tight around your finger, *softly* wiggle it, adding a slow twist or two, or just leave your

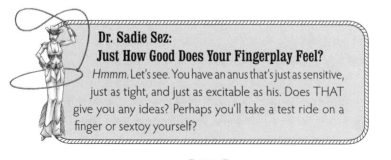

Dr. Sadie Sez:
Just How Good Does Your Fingerplay Feel?

Hmmm. Let's see. You have an anus that's just as sensitive, just as tight, and just as excitable as his. Does THAT give you any ideas? Perhaps you'll take a test ride on a finger or sextoy yourself?

finger still so his muscles can relax around it. The further in you go, the fewer nerve endings you'll find, which means he'll start responding more to pressure and rhythm than the touch and vibration that works so well closer to the entrance.

🐾 **Touch his spot.** As soon as your second knuckle disappears inside, curl your finger toward his belly button, and feel around for a firm, round bulb that feels like the tip of a nose. That's his HE-spot!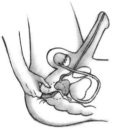

🐾 **Pleasure his spot.** Using slow, gentle, "come here"-type curling motions, fingertip his HE-spot with the same pressure you'd use to rub your own eyeball. Run your fingertip all around till you find what he likes—up-down, side-to-side, off-center. Don't stop your oral loving or handjob, either.

🐾 **Talk to the spot.** Check in with him: *faster? slower? softer? harder?* (but not too hard). Keep stroking his penis or playing with his balls, too. You'll know you've got it right when his legs spread wider, his breathing gets faster, he's moaning or screaming and riding your finger like the stud he is.

🐾 **Bring it on.** Whisper "Show me how you like it" and let him move on your now-motionless finger. Remember, unlike your

G-spot, his HE-spot doesn't need as much rigorous stimulation—and the right touch can trigger huge orgasms, even if he doesn't have an erection.

🐾 **Rest your finger.** Try a prostate stimulator. These are toys curved to stimulate his prostate and vibrate him to new spectacular orgasms. Or try a strap-on with a dildo ("pegging") for advanced HE-spot loving (see chapter 18).

Not Gonna Do It?
You've Got An Alternative

If he's too squeamish to let you slip your finger inside, you can actually stimulate his prostate from *outside* his body—and although it probably won't give him an orgasm, it'll still feel great.

Drizzle some sex lube onto two or three of your fingertips, and press them gently into his taint (*perineum*). You can also make a loose fist and rub lightly with your knuckles, directing your pressure up toward the base of his penis. Try circular strokes or back-and-forth pressure till you find what he likes. Simultaneously wrap your mouth or your other hand around his penis, and bring him to an explosive orgasm.

Dr. Sadie Sez: One Step At A Time.
If you're a newcomer to prostate play, and some of these techniques seem a little too advanced for you, start with my book *Tickle His Pickle—Your Hands-On Guide To Penis Pleasing*, available at ticklekitty.com.

Kissing Butt
The thrilling 3-part warm-up to prostate play: a flick, a lick, and milk his dick.

Uranus Landing
With all the excitement from her grand oral love, any jitters about HE-spot play melt away as her lubed finger slides inside.

Rocket Launcher

A well-lubed finger
curves upward toward
the base of his penis,
while her other hand is
busy teasing and
tantalizing, too.

Moon Probe

Handjob for
him. Comfort for her. Lube
for all.

Strap-On I:
Winged Pleasure

With his legs hooked over her hips, she's now aimed for perfect insertion, his legs propped for full thrusting power, and her hand positioned for plenty of loving touch.

Strap-On II:
Bareback Rider

HE-spot pleasure, self-pleasure, and orgasmic prostate pleasure—all in one!

Strap-On III:
The Dominator

HE-spot orgasms and an overpowering sense of domination—for very special couples only.

13 Voluptuous Lovin'

The earth may not be getting smaller, but a lot of its inhabitants are getting larger. If you are one of these voluptuous adults, you're surely tired of hearing about fad diets, body image concerns and the latest health warnings.

You'd rather talk about sex—and start enjoying it more!

While every adult has sexual desires, those who are *not* plus-size can never completely relate to many of the lovemaking challenges you face. However, as you'll often find, a creative solution or ingenious workaround may be what you need to enjoy all of the sexual passion you and your partner deserve.

As always, the best solution is to begin with your mouth—and initiate an open, honest talk with your lover. If you can't figure out how to begin, just take a pen and circle this paragraph for the simplest conversation starter ever!

Throughout this guidebook, you'll find plenty of stimulating ideas to bring into your discussion—and even more solutions within this chapter to assist with your specific position questions. So don't put off hotter sex any longer: *talk*.

Cowgirls Only!
Plus Size Can Be A Plus

One of our species' strongest and most powerful sexual turn-ons may surprise you: *confidence*. While body image issues and years of distasteful societal conditioning may attempt to sour your spirit, bringing renewed sexual confidence to bed with you can lift passions to exciting new highs.

When you open yourself to a healthier worldview, you may discover that some of what's inhibiting you may actually be turning on your lover. Your sensual softness is much more sexually exciting

Dr. Sadie Sez: Sex Techniques Of The Voluptuous: REVEALED!

As more and more plus-size adults and their lovers come forward with their sexual desires, the adult video industry is happy to oblige them. Now you can find a wide spectrum of adult-themed DVDs of plus-size women and men that you can enjoy for more than their erotic thrills—you can see how others approach the positions and situations you may have always wondered about. See what sex with confidence looks like. Giggle. Learn. Be empowered!

than you imagine. A feature of your body is a favorite fascination your lover can't resist. Certain sexual positions play right into your lover's fantasies about being restrained. *Who knew?*

Opening a dialog demonstrates your self-confidence and self-worth, which is sexy to every lover in the world, yours included.

Cowgirls & Cowboys!
Supersized Sex's Biggest Secret

There's a terrific product you can easily get that will help your creativity in bed, assist with balance, relieve stress on knees, elbows and other joints, and give you some of the most satisfying orgasms ever.

They're called pillows, and the more you use, the better you'll feel.

Try placing smaller pillows under the head, neck, and elbows for spot-elevation, and larger pillows to align and support other parts of your bodies. If the pillows on the bed now don't quite do the trick, take a field trip to a home decor or department store to creatively match their shapes to your needs. Try square or rectangular throw pillows, U-shaped neck-rest pillows, blow-up air pillows, round-roll pillows, full-body pillows, bolsters, memory foam pillows, you name it!

Then race back home and place them strategically around your bodies for the most balanced, comfortable sex of your lives.

No-Ouch Couch

The cushioned couch is a top spot for lovin'—with pillows and bolsters always within easy reach to support your flexing joints.

Deep Mission

Toss the backrest cushions and create some space to spread open wider than ever for deep-seated Missionary penetration.

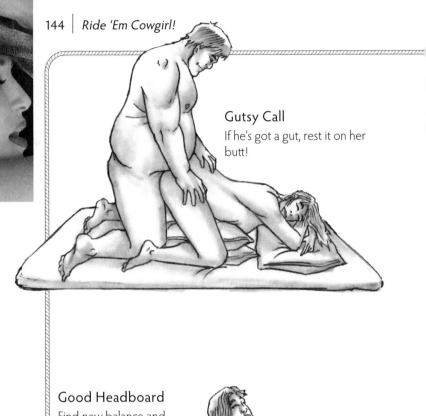

Gutsy Call
If he's got a gut, rest it on her butt!

Good Headboard
Find new balance and support by grabbing hold of the headboard, because the added leverage speeds up the action.

14 Pregnant Poses

Cowgirls Only!

Cowboys: See you at page 151.

Congratulations…you're pregnant!

If you're hoping to learn more about taking care of your baby, pick up a leading baby care book. This chapter's about taking care of YOU, baby!

When enjoyed as directed, sex during pregnancy is healthy for you, safe for your baby, and primal for your horndog partner. By exploring the ideas on the next few pages, you'll keep your passions glowing hot and crazy, while your bun-in-the-oven stays warm and cozy.

May your journey into parenthood be filled with wonder, joy, laughter…and many eye-popping orgasms!

Hop On The Hormone Rollercoaster

You're horny. You're cranky. You're sleepy. You're giddy. You're up. You're down. You're whirling out on a wicked loop-de-loop ride. Or not.

How will pregnancy affect you? You'll be the first to know. But be prepared: the very same hormones you produce to nurture your baby and prime your body for the birth can also whip up a wild sex-drive ride.

So strap on your seat belt and steer toward this advice: trust your body to tell you what it wants *right now*—then share your needs with your partner during "what feels good *today*" discussions. You'll do more than set a positive tone for your entire pregnancy. You'll strengthen your long-term commitment to each other—and to your new baby.

Play It Safe, For Baby's Sake!

Is intercourse safe during pregnancy? Ask your physician, and don't be shy—be specific. Chances are if you're having a normal, healthy pregnancy, the answer is yes. (Everything except the chandelier-

swinging, that is!) And you can be assured that intercourse is safe right up until your water breaks, or until labor begins.

But NEVER engage in sex when:

✔ **Your physician advises against it.**

✔ **You are bleeding or leaking fluid.**

✔ **Your water has broken.**

✔ **One of you has an active sexually transmitted disease.**

✔ **You have a history of premature birth or labor (unless your physician gives you the okay).**

✔ **Your physician says your placenta is covering the opening of your cervix.**

If your health situation changes suddenly, or you have medical questions or concerns—STOP—and contact your physician immediately!

First Trimester: Sex Takes A Holiday

Toss out the contraception—you've conceived! Now you can dive right in for all the carefree sex you've always dreamed of, without pills, foams, caps, sponges, jellies, diaphragms, condoms or worries.

Carefree, that is, until morning sickness, crankifying exhaustion, sore "don't-touch-me" breasts and raging hormones suck the fun right out of you.

Guess what? That's normal! Intercourse will just have to take a back-seat for now. But look at your partner: He's not hurtin'—he's horny! How about trying some of the other sexy activities you can enjoy besides intercourse—like the outercourse fun in chapter 15.

Second Trimester: Pregnancy's Honeymoon

Who flipped on the sex switch? And why is it set to "insatiable?"

Your hormones have now re-blended for the second phase of your pregnancy, sending pure sex fuel racing throughout your entire body, and creating physical changes destined to supercharge your sexual appetite:

♥ **Surge of blood flowing to your vagina**

♥ **Larger, more sensitive labia**

♥ **Increase in natural lubrication**

♥ **Bigger, more voluptuous breasts**

♥ **Heightened nipple sensations**

If you've never orgasmed in your life, you may now become unstoppable. And if you were already orgasmic, the lid could fly off for indescribably longer, deeper, wilder *and even multiple* waves of orgasmic ecstasy! Of course, your mileage may vary.

Why is this happening? Some say this surge of orgasmic energy at just the right time in baby's development is part of the plan to create healthier, happier, more fun-loving offspring. And who are we to argue with Mother Nature?

So listen to your body. Treat your baby (and yourself!) to the wealth of natural pleasure endorphins you both deserve. And at about the fourth month, try some new positions other than Missionary—it can crimp the flow of blood to the baby.

Third Trimester: Getting Over The Hump

Are you creative? You'd better be—because fitting yourselves around a ballooning belly is going to take all your imagination.

But that's not the only sexual hurdle facing soon-to-be parents. Many women cease feeling attractive, even though their partners often see them as wildly sexy. The solution? Accept your physical changes as inevitable, and revel in the magical feeling of a new life growing inside you. Then you'll find it easier to agree with your

> ### Dr. Sadie Sez:
> ### Are You Feeling Guilty Just Lying There?
> That's okay—let your partner do most of the work. You're carrying a growing baby (and that's work, too!). Remind him you'll return to being his energetic sex partner again soon after the birth. Until then, just relax and enjoy.

partner and enjoy this beautiful stage together. So stay playful and be careful—especially if your sex drive flips into high gear now.

Positions (And Pillows) With A Purpose

Your rapidly growing tummy will put Missionary out of reach for now, but you can still enjoy all the pleasures of Doggystyle, Cowgirl and Spooning.

How do you cope with all that physical awkwardness? Pillows! Just place them strategically around you to reduce strain on hands and knees, for support under your belly, to balance out your body, as well as to raise up your torso for the perfect penetration angle. And if need be, borrow a few pillows off the living room couch, and it'll feel like you're having sex on a cloud!

Cowboys Only!
Be Her Superhero—Here's How

Funny thing about being with a pregnant woman: some days she'll turn you on like you're her prize racing stud—and other days she'll wave you off like you're a pushy panhandler. During those "off" days, try to remind yourself that her ever-changing hormones are completely in charge. Not her. Not you.

What to do? Be kind. Act respectfully. Don't mutter. Don't pressure her. Kiss her on the forehead. Remind yourself she'll come around. And if your little head keeps talking back to your big head, disappear with a glossy magazine and a tube o' lube.

What else can you do?

- **Massage her.** Often. And all over. Trust her when she says her feet, lower back and shoulders ache. Lend a hand for 10 or 20 minutes. After all, she's carrying your child around 24/7.

- **Wow her.** Are you surprising yourself with vivid daydreams about ravishing your glowing, growing partner? Are you taken

aback by how truly beautiful she looks? Then tell her—clearly and often.

- **Buzz her.** What if you were to surprise her with a thoughtful gift: a small clitoral vibrator. What if you then bring her to orgasm after orgasm? What if this keeps things pleasant and calm around the house?

- **Relish her.** As her body grows more voluptuous, you'll find she's got a few surprises in store for you: tighter, slipperier, juicier, hornier sex— especially during the second trimester— with no need for birth control. Isn't life great?

Sex-During-Pregnancy FAQ

Will sex dent the baby's forehead?

Nope! Mother Nature carefully ensures that the baby is completely sealed and cushioned inside the fluid-filled amniotic sac. Thankfully, your penis will never touch the baby. Nor will any of your fluids. And no, the baby isn't watching!

Can sex cause a miscarriage?

Nope! Not during a normal pregnancy. Don't worry. Enjoy yourselves.

> **Dr. Sadie Sez:**
> **Be A Lean, Clean Sex Machine. Always.**
> Here's how to keep unwanted germs away from your baby. Before *and after* sex, be sure to thoroughly lather your hands, sextoys and midsection with antibacterial soap under hot running water.

Is it safe to perform cunnilingus?

Yes! And thanks to her swelling labia and increased lubrication, there's more to love. But NEVER blow air into the vagina—it can create an extremely hazardous situation for mother and child.

Is it okay for her to orgasm?

Yes! Orgasms are perfectly safe, but can trigger small contractions. This is normal during a healthy pregnancy. But if the contractions are strong, and last more than 30 minutes, call your physician immediately.

Is anal sex safe?

Yes! It's a good alternative to vaginal sex, but hemorrhoid irritation can put an end to your fun. Always stop if there's any discomfort, and abide by all the safety rules in the Appendix—especially about not transferring bacteria into the vagina.

Sex In Postpartum Times

Welcome to your new life as proud parents with a newborn in the house. If you're not thoroughly exhausted from baby care, as well as parenting any other kids, bill paying, food shopping, cooking, cleaning and wage earning, you may ask yourselves:

Where, exactly, does sex fit on this list?

Physically, most doctors recommend waiting six weeks before restarting your sex life, whether birth was vaginal or by C-section. Emotionally, it may take a bit longer to equalize hormone levels that inspire sexual desire.

Until then, find your intimacies in other ways. Try brief, loving "check in" phone calls, as well as flirtatious emails and text messages throughout the day. Initiate loving make-out sessions. Take hot showers with each other during baby's naptime. And most of all, talk about how you're feeling.

When the time is right to restart your sex life, ease into it gradually. Pleasure each other orally, or by hand, until you're *both* comfortable with penetration. And Mom, please remember:

♥ **You're still fertile.** Even if you're breastfeeding and haven't yet had your first period. Use contraception.

♥ **Breastfeeding can lead to vaginal dryness.** Apply a good water-based sex lube. If you're also feeling un-elastic or experiencing discomfort, consult your physician; there are medications that may help.

♥ **Normal vaginal size will return.** If this was your first child, tightness usually returns within eight weeks after delivery. If you've had two or more births, return time and size will vary.

♥ **Sex with baby in the room is okay.** Your little angel will never know! And your sounds of lovemaking are reassuring that you're nearby.

♥ **Don't forget toys for YOU.** Especially the vibrating kind!

♥ **Laugh at leaks!** You may expel breast milk during sex. So don't be surprised. It's unavoidable. Just enjoy.

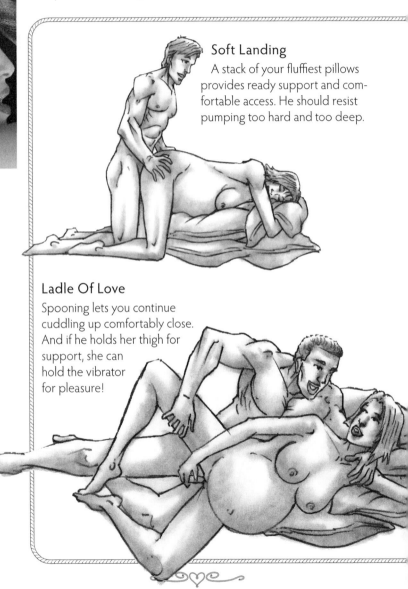

Soft Landing

A stack of your fluffiest pillows provides ready support and comfortable access. He should resist pumping too hard and too deep.

Ladle Of Love

Spooning lets you continue cuddling up comfortably close. And if he holds her thigh for support, she can hold the vibrator for pleasure!

Magic Spoon

For pure comfort and heavenly
sensations, she places her top leg
back over his, and his penis
and fingers deliver the
magic.

Cloud 9

Her tummy on the pillows,
his fingertips on her clitoris,
like sex in the clouds.

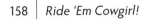

Balancing Ball

For better control and balance, she tucks her feet over his inner thighs—then both gyrate in small circles. Can you still reach each other's lips?

Prone to Please

His shoulders resting on pillows,
her hands braced on his chest,
everyone's centered and stable
when passion gets hot and playful.

Golden Gate

Clasping hands eases the pressure so she can stay perfectly still
while he thrusts skyward.

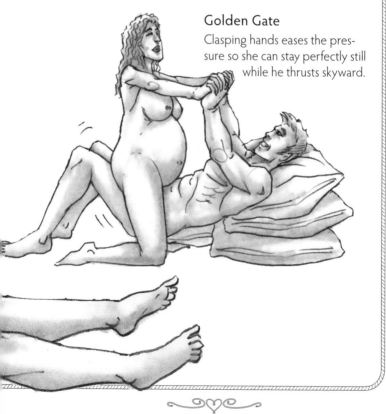

Belly Up

Brace yourselves for pleasure with shallower penetration—a headboard or wall creates a protective angle that also allows him to reach around and touch her softly.

Wheelbarrow

Cozy. Comfy. Easy on mommy.

Outercourse: Good Messy Fun

15

$\mathbb{W}$hat do you call intercourse without the "in"? Outercourse, of course!

Outercourse takes the penetration out of sex—but not the fun. You still enjoy deeply sensual, skin-on-skin lovemaking. You still share a thrilling physical connection. And you still experience explosive, scream-worthy orgasms.

So why would anybody ever want to forgo the deep satisfaction of vaginal or anal pen-etration? Because sometimes, intercourse just isn't on the menu—or you'd simply rather enjoy a total out-of-body experience.

Exciting! Exhilarating! Safer! Convenient!

Outercourse offers something for everybody. If you're a virgin, you stay a virgin. If you're abstinent, you stay un-penetrated. And if you're both experienced, you can recharge your love life by redis-covering the joys of starting over.

Consider these practical reasons, too: Since the penis doesn't enter the vagina, the risk of pregnancy and STIs goes way down, while your freedom and enjoyment go way up.

What's more, you can still be intimate if you're not ready for intercourse, she's menstruating, or one of you is too tired. You also have a no-risk solution if you've run out of condoms, misplaced the diaphragm or forgotten The Pill. You can even silence a squeaky bed if your eavesdropping in-laws are right next door.

Dr. Sadie Sez: Less Risk Doesn't Mean No Risk.
ANY sexual contact between humans means risk—even low-risk outercourse. Keep semen from splashing near the vagina, mucous membranes and open cuts. Practice safer sex during oral sex. See the Appendix for more vital safer sex guidelines.

Outercourse: A Tit For A Tat

Outercourse offers each of you a new way to express yourself creatively as you learn more about each other sexually.

When he drifts off to dreamland after his orgasm, she may still be ready, willing and surging for another orgasm or three. Next time, if he tries these thrilling outercourse techniques and learns more about her desires, both partners can drift off to dreamland together, totally satisfied and deliciously spent.

On the flipside, when she isn't in the mood, and his sex drive is in overdrive, she can get him off with some of these tempting outercourse techniques before sending him off to dreamland happy and content.

Come Awaken Your Sexual Creativity!

Take a holiday from the finer techniques of penetration and explore the erotic nooks and crannies of your lover's body with much greater intimacy.

♥ **Kiss.** Seduce with your lips and tongue: Peck. Lick. Lip-lock. Flick. Entwine. Go soft, hard, slow, gentle, mellow, deep—then work

Dr. Sadie Sez: A Young Woman's Intimacy Insurance Policy.

It's easy to get sucked into the sex game before you're physically and emotionally ready—especially its hurtful side. Outercourse offers you a way to go at your own pace (not his!), and absorb what's happening to you before it can become overwhelming. Take him for fun outercourse "test drives" as you get to know each other better. It's not just smarter, it's safer.

up to hot, wet and messy! Hold your lover's chin. Caress your lover's face. Pretend it's oral sex at its best.

♥ **Dry hump.** Rub your clothed bodies together lustily in the backyard, in a restaurant coatroom or on the backseat of your car. Steer clear of rough fabrics and jagged zippers on sensitive spots.

♥ **Fingerplay.** Unleash those living sextoys in your pockets— your hands! Wrap, stroke, jerk, caress, rub, stimulate—you know where. Take turns, or pleasure each other simultaneously. Or watch each other do unto yourselves.

♥ **Massage.** Coat your lover's most intimate spots with a little massage oil and explore behind the ears, down the neck, down the back, around the butt, and behind the knees.

♥ **Penis pleasure hunt.** Seek out her body's most sensual spots with his heat-seeking penis! Drizzle on some sex lube and slide it between her breasts, thighs, armpits, inner elbow fold, feet—any soft warm inviting skin (just not the vagina or anus, Romeo!).

♥ **Toy around.** Reach into your sextoy chest and pull out a few of your favorites: feathers, vibrators, dildos, lubes, warming oils—or slip an erotic video into your DVD. Toy chest empty? Time to surprise your lover with a special batteries-included gift.

♥ **Back door reach around.** Tease slowly toward the pleasure-center of your lover's butt with your fingers, mouth and toys—but remember to use latex barriers when you reach the prize.

♥ **Play games.** Play out your fantasies and fetishes; wear costumes, wigs, stiletto heels, or sexy lingerie, then grind together to a steamy song and bring each other to orgasm while your clothes are still on!

♥ **Get oral.** Let your lips do the talking as you take turns tasting and licking each other with gusto. Or change it up and get into the "69" position and delight each other simultaneously.

16

Location!
Location!
Location!

$\mathbb{D}$o you ever hear your mattress going, *"Boing, Boing, Boing?"* Could it really be telling you, *Boring, Boring, Boring?"*

Maybe it's time to give that old bed a rest. After all, you live in a big world with lots of nooks and crannies for daring lovemaking.

Right now, peer over the top of this book. How many potential places do you see, near and far, hidden and not-so-hidden, that you and your lover could slip into—or onto—for the most mischievous sex of your lives?

There's No Place Like Home

Where in your home have you *never* made love? Once you've narrowed that long list down to your top erotic few, make a plan to pack off the kids, turn off the phones, pull down the shades, and get ready to party!

Try the guest bed, shower, bath, countertop, staircase, weight bench, home office or washing machine (while it's on!). Or venture out to the backyard, deck or balcony, swimming pool, or even up against the car (parked *inside!*).

Be spontaneous and act out role-plays in your new locales. You'll plant private erotic memories throughout your home—ready to recall during parties when friends sit unwittingly in the heat of your X-rated flashbacks!

Sex In The Great Outdoors

If you fantasize about making love by a tropical waterfall or under a starry sky—or even on the swings at your local playground—

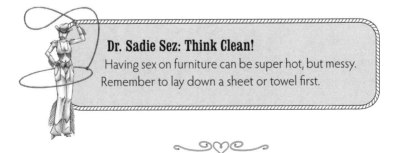

Dr. Sadie Sez: Think Clean!
Having sex on furniture can be super hot, but messy. Remember to lay down a sheet or towel first.

> ### Dr. Sadie Sez: Anything Goes—Almost!
> Your home is designed more for living than loving, so watch out for hazards that can quickly turn ecstasy into agony: wobbly tables and burning candles, slippery shower tiles, burn-your-knees rugs, unreinforced balcony railings, no-parking-brake office chairs. Please be careful!

sex outdoors can actually breathe new romantic life into the most mattress-bound relationship.

Alfresco sex, or making love outside, is not for everyone, and certainly not for every time, but most people agree it can satisfy a deeply primal urge that's very, very exciting—especially if you choose the right time and place.

Secluded Sex, Alfresco Style

Living on a planet of 6.6 billion people somehow limits the number of suitable places for private outdoor sex, especially for city dwellers. The solution is simply to sacrifice a bit of spontaneity to enjoy the seclusion you seek.

Time for an erotic picnic! Pack a soft blanket or sheet, a few bottles of water, your favorite wine, trusty corkscrew, a bit of finger food and a pocketful of condoms, and venture into the woods or onto a secluded rooftop.

Bring a flashlight for nighttime fun at the beach, golf course, playground or park. For extra camouflage, bring a blanket that blends into the color of the ground, which can also double as a lightning-fast cover-up in a pinch!

Exhibitionist Sex, Alfresco Style

If you're aroused by the thought of being caught by strangers who can do nothing but watch, choose locations that offer good sightlines, buffered by distance or natural barriers—like up on a balcony, out on a fire escape, on a rugged hillside, or on a rooftop ringed by taller buildings.

If greater risk is your thrill, seek out up-close places where you can offer unwitting passersby a real erotic eyeful. Parking lot staircases, alleyways, elevators, bathrooms, park benches, changing rooms, taxi backseats, ferry boat rides, library stacks, hotel hallways, darkened movie theaters, beaches, coves, empty classrooms, coat check rooms—the earth's the limit!

Dr. Sadie Sez: Alfresco Sex In A Zip.
If she "forgets" to wear panties under her skirt, and he somehow "neglects" to wear his boxers, passions can zoom from zero to sixty as fast as you can say, "Zzzzzip…"

> ## Dr. Sadie Sez: Roughing It Can Get Rough.
> Moving your lovemaking outside means giving up the many comforts of the great indoors. So be careful to avoid these hazards:
>
> Spiders, mosquitoes, biting bugs, poisons ivy, oak and sumac, stinging nettles, hungry or protective animals, gravel rash, prickly straw, irritating grains of sand in sensitive crevices, sharp grass blades, waterborne germs from lakes, streams and hot springs, and unexpected automatic water sprinklers. *Have a good time!*

Getting Caught, Alfresco Style

Is the *thought* of getting caught more thrilling than the reality?

If your naked passions are uncovered by someone you know, plan on being the butt of punchlines for years to come. If you're discovered by law enforcement, plan on a stern warning, a fine, or even jail time. And if you're observed by a total stranger, well then, plan on having your thrill fulfilled!

Deep in the woods, you may not be as alone as you think either— you could be discovered by a hungry bear or other wild critter. Double-seal used condoms in plastic bags, and dispose of them properly with your trash. Don't bury them in the ground, don't burn

them in the fire, and don't store them in your tent—they actually give off an attracting scent.

If you're enjoying sex in the city, you could easily be detected by cameras recording your every move, much to the delight of bored security guards who can't wait to upload to YouTube!

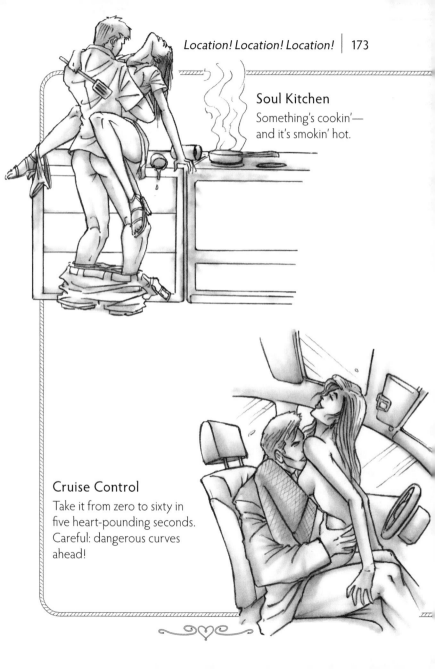

Soul Kitchen
Something's cookin'—
and it's smokin' hot.

Cruise Control
Take it from zero to sixty in
five heart-pounding seconds.
Careful: dangerous curves
ahead!

The Sexerciser

Hop aboard for the ultimate cardio workout.

Desk Job

Here's a reason to keep your workplace clear. Or try it on a conference table for a meeting you'll never forget.

Pie In The Sky
Enjoy that first-class upgrade you wanted.

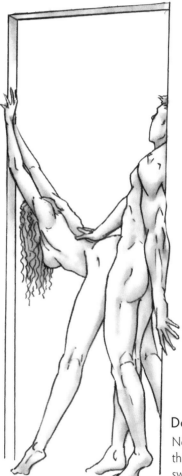

Door Jammin'
No matter how you grasp the knob and push, this is swingin'.

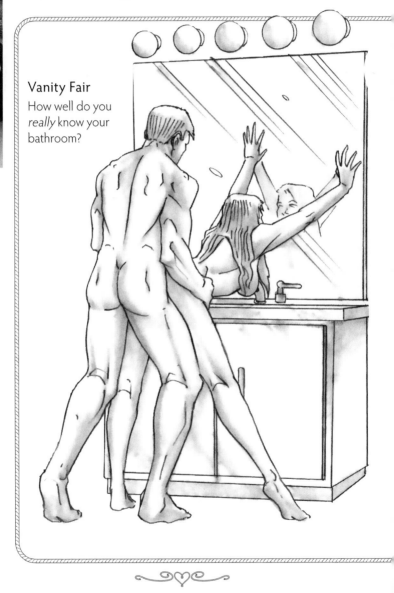

Vanity Fair
How well do you *really* know your bathroom?

The Jolly Forester

Finding wood in the great outdoors was never so easy— or so satisfying.

Stairway To Heaven

Sometimes you just can't wait until you get home. Not recommended on escalators.

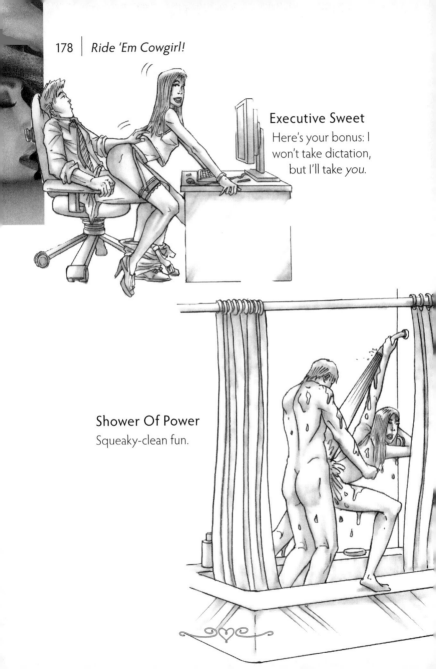

Executive Sweet
Here's your bonus: I
won't take dictation,
but I'll take *you*.

Shower Of Power
Squeaky-clean fun.

17 Vive La Différence

Waiting with breathless anticipation as a new lover strips down to birthday-suit reality is like unwrapping a gift: You hope you like what you get, and pray that it fits.

If you're lucky, your naked bodies and erotic hotspots will come together in a wet, wild, made-for-each-other orgasmic embrace.

If not, you're *still* lucky, but lovemaking's going take a little extra magic.

That's sex: No guarantees. No test drives. What's in the jeans is what's in the genes. And whether you're mating for a nighttime—or a lifetime—that divine head-to-toe match-up you want can easily be achieved through a bit of erotic repositioning and technique touch-up.

After all, you can both have a lot of fun turning up what turns you on, and turning down whatever doesn't. And that's a gift worth unwrapping.

Cowgirls Only!
The Penis Monologues

Did you know all penises have memories? Not for scientific facts or baseball trivia, but simply for position and place.

Every time a guy gets an erection, his penis returns to the exact size, shape and elevation as the last time—as well as every time after that—with only some lessening in intensity over his lifetime.

This means that the erection he gets is the erection you get.

Most women can be very happy with a penis of just about any size and shape, as long as the guy attached to it is a passionate and generous lover. Yet if your partner's penis isn't necessarily your ultimate choice, your solution is simple: custom tailor his special shape to the lusty moves and positions now at your fingertips.

COWGIRL BONUS SECTION

Beef-Up Fun With Any Penis Type!

Come take this peek-in-the-pants tour and match your lover's erection style to these rave positions.

Average

A hard-working, well-proportioned penis can barely be considered "average"—yet that's exactly what it's known as *statistically.*

While surveys vary, and guys have been known to exaggerate, experts agree the average penis measures between 2 to 4 inches soft, and 5 to 7 inches hard, with an erect circumference of about 4 to 5 inches. The size of a soft penis has practically no bearing on its size when hard—a small soft penis can grow huge, while a long soft one may simply grow stiff.

Rave Positions. Any and all.

Longer

Big, versatile and gasp-worthy, you can enjoy most any position with this jumbo-sized model that's a full 7 inches or longer. Expect glorious G-spot stimulation and little chance of surprise "slip outs." But be careful: his hard, deep thrusting can strike your cervix at the back of your vagina. While some women find this pleasurable, others may experience discomfort, pain and even cervical injury. If so, stop right away—then limit his depth by changing positions, or slip a penis buffer on him to automatically shorten his reach.

Rave Positions. *Cowgirl* and *Reverse Cowgirl:* You're in full control of the thrusting depth, which brings pleasure and comfort together in one. *Missionary:* Close your thighs so his legs are outside yours. *Standing up:* His pornstar penis can actually bend around curves!

Shorter

Contrary to popular belief, many women prefer a lover who isn't hung like a horse—especially if you have a shorter vaginal canal or you're a newcomer to intercourse. And you can even treat him to a heart-pounding thrill that his longneck brethren will probably never experience: full stern-to-stem deep throat oral sex!

Rave Positions. *Missionary:* He'll know exactly how far he can out-stroke without any surprise "pop outs." Try experimenting with leg positioning for the best deeper penetration angles (see page 49). *Cowgirl:* Take control yourself and keep your up-and-down stroking shallow, or sit and gyrate, grinding your clitoris gloriously into his soft, sensual pubic mound.

Thicker

For that satisfying feeling of fullness, many women crave a thick, girthy model—even if he's not particularly long. His extra circumference pleasure-stretches your vagina with each delicious stroke for a "hurts-so-good" feeling of fullness that can skyrocket your satisfaction.

Rave Positions. Any and all! Be sure to warm up first with some sizzling outercourse play (and maybe a clitoral orgasm or two). Work in his penis slowly, and be sure you're always naturally well-lubricated, or drizzle on some slippery sex lube, and reapply as often as needed.

Thinner

If you have an extra-tight vagina, or you're into anal sex, or you simply prefer less girth, you'll find that less circumference equals greater

pleasure. If you wish to add girth, slip a penis thickener on him to give you that feeling of fullness. Or try Kegel exercises to tighten your pelvic muscles so you can squeeze more tightly on his shaft. You may even want to try on an exhilarating butt plug that will narrow your vaginal canal from within.

Rave Positions. *Missionary and Spooning:* You'll find more tightness and friction when your legs are closed and pressed together.

Banana

Quite possibly, the world's most perfect penis! With a graceful arc, its gentle curve aims directly for your glorious G-spot, so every thrust reminds you that you're making love to a living sextoy.

Rave Positions. If he curves north, *Missionary.* If he arcs south, *Doggystyle.* If he slopes east or west, *Spooning* will let you swerve into his curve.

Bolted

Like a fireplug anchored in cement, once this model comes to full attention, there's no "play" in this penis whatsoever—all the play comes from *you!* Since he's swivel-less and stands at atten-HUT,

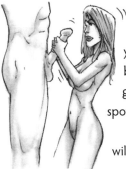

you always know when to salute. You may not
be able to bring off Reverse Cowgirl, but he's
guaranteed to stay in place for most pleasure
spot focus, so ride 'em cowgirl!

　　Rave Positions. Any and all his rigid angle
will allow.

Springy

Think of this model like an amusement thrill park ride—taking
you on a full 360-degrees of whirlwind action
that'll match your wildest gyrations, always
ready to stop exactly where you want. Hop
on and give it a spin—but be sure to guide
this swivel-ly erection inside with an assist
from your hand.

　　Rave Positions. *Reverse Cowgirl.* Or
Standing up. Or *standing Doggystyle.*
Or with him *sitting in a chair.*

Uncircumcised

Lots of guys don't have foreskins because in many cultures they're
removed during infancy (*circumcision*). A foreskin is simply a hood
of skin that covers and protects the head of the penis. Foreskins
come in varying lengths, and during erections they may be visible,
but most will stretch back and "disappear." Women may express

a visual preference, but there's usually no difference in sensation for you once he's inside. However, you want to make sure he keeps himself clean under there, since bacteria love hiding in all the nooks and crannies.

Rave Positions. Any and all! But please remember: the foreskin is thin and delicate, and can tear easily. Never grip it too hard, or stretch it too fast or too far. Be sure he's well-lubed, too.

Your Vagina: A Beautiful Unfolding Story

Mirror, mirror on the floor; who's the fairest of them all?

Too few women ever gaze at their own vaginas, and even fewer have seen how erotic and elegant they look while aroused.

Most guys know, of course. Even if they've never been with a woman, luscious labial close-ups of every size and shape are never more than a few web clicks away. And they all agree: the vagina is one of the most heavenly sights on the planet. Come. Take a closer look.

The Vaginal Variations

Vaginas are as varied as the sizes and shapes of human mouths. The outer lips can be small, big, flat, long, puffy, proportional—or not. The inner lips come in various shapes too, and can even protrude beyond the outer lips. The clitoris can be big and round or small and hidden. And the overall color can be anything from light pink to dark red. Whatever the genetic make-up, each is unique, and each is beautiful.

During arousal, everything springs to life. Labia bloom like petals of a flower. The clitoris may grow slightly, often emerging out of hiding to seek delicious stimulation. The vagina lengthens, as well as stretches or tightens to hug an incoming penis, becoming slippery-wet with natural lubricant. Even the colors grow more intense as the entire region floods with warm, rich blood.

What about *your* vagina? If you've haven't lifted a hand mirror to look at yours, your self-visualization may be based solely on airbrushed images from adult magazines, or simply on what you *imagine* it looks like. If you're curious and comfortable, why not admire your own beauty, even watching yourself as you grow more and more excited. Learning this about yourself, and sharing these discoveries with your loving partner, can inspire genuine passion and new intensity in your lovemaking.

Fitting Positions For Every Vaginal Style

🧘 **Extra tight.** Vaginal tightness can be genetic, or caused by being nervous, self-conscious, disconnected, or just not being ready. Often, it's due to dryness. Try drizzling a good sex lube all over his penis as well as your vagina, and enjoy plenty of foreplay and clitoral stimulation. When you feel ready, gradually insert one lubed finger, then two, and feel if your vagina is stretching comfortably. If so, touch his lubed penis to your vaginal opening and begin slow penetration. If there's continued difficulty or pain, or penetration is not possible, give it a rest and talk to your physician. It's nothing to be embarrassed about—enjoying a healthy sex life is worth it.

Rave Positions. Once you're well-lubed and comfortable, and proceeding slowly, any and all!

🧘 **Not tight enough.** Excess lubrication can actually create a looser fit. Try wiping away your natural lube with a soft washcloth or disposable wipe before (and during) lovemaking. You can also insert a finger or two, or even a small dildo, alongside his penis during intercourse. Tightening your pelvic muscles with Kegel exercises will help, too.

Rave Positions. Spooning: As you press your thighs together, you'll create extra tightness. *Modified Doggystyle:* Lay flat on your stomach with your legs straight out and positioned between his legs for a snug, thigh-hugging fit.

🐞 **Shallow.** If you have a shorter vaginal canal, the head of his penis may bump your cervix with every thrust. While this can be highly stimulating for some women, it can cause discomfort, or even cervical injury for others. Stop immediately if you feel discomfort or pain. Make sure you're fully aroused before penetration, to give your vaginal canal time to expand and extend to its full length. If you still feel discomfort, treat him to a penis buffer.

    Rave Positions. *Cowgirl:* You're in control of the thrusting, so you can limit the depth to your own comfort. *Spooning:* Your butt can act as a soft, natural buffer to prevent deep penetration without inhibiting pleasure. *Standing:* The vertical angle can also limit his penetration depth.

🐞 **Too wet.** The good news: You save money on sex lube! But too much self-lubrication can also create a feeling of looseness, which can lead to a loss of sensation. Try wiping yourselves with a soft washcloth before (and during) intercourse. You may also choose to bypass extended foreplay and enjoy the excitement of jump-right-into-it sex—before an abundance natural juices begin to flow.

    Rave Positions. Any and all, with a soft washcloth or disposable wipe within easy reach.

🐞 **Not wet enough.** Dryness doesn't necessarily mean you're not aroused. Self-lubrication can also be hampered by estrogen

levels, stress, time of the month, menopause, prescription drugs, cold remedies, certain birth control pills, alcohol, marijuana—even extended lovemaking. The solution? Sex lube—and not the icky institutional stuff, but a smooth, sensual, silky lube created exclusively for your pleasure. Try lube shooters (see page 200) for longer, deeper slipperiness.

Rave Positions. Any and all, with a bottle of sex lube within easy reach.

18 Sexy Playthings

What if they designed a bed just for sex? How would it zig? How would it zag? And most importantly, how would you ever get out of it to go to work?

Every year, folks in the sextoy business turn out hundreds of new ways to buzz, twirl and shake your love life awake. Sexy playthings now come in every style, shape, texture and color for you to try in bed, out of bed, in public, with intercourse or anal play—even by remote control!

Gone are the days of creepy dismal downtown sex stores. Now you can get anything you want in private on the web, in friendly boutiques filled with colorful toys and slinky lingerie, or at fun-filled sextoy parties at a trusted friend's house.

191

In fact, your choices today are so vast, the only challenge is knowing which products are designed to satisfy your own true desires.

Position Is Everything

To add variety, a lot more pleasure, and even a few shared laughs as you tumble naked toward ecstasy, why not add a body positioner or two into your bedroom repertoire?

♥ **Sex furniture.** Designed to contour to your aroused bodies, these wedges, pillows, couches and chairs position you for new erotic angles and elevations. Without gravity to fight, and with ease of access guaranteed, you're free to pursue pure orgasmic pleasures.

♥ **Swing sets.** Go airborne! Just screw a sex swing securely into a doorframe or ceiling beam (or get a portable stand), and enjoy gravity-defying fun with freedom of movement, deeper penetration and wild visuals. Order one with a bungee cord and experience bouncy "basket trick" pleasures.

♥ **Sling sets.** Like invisible hands holding her legs aloft, this sex sling takes all the strain out of Missionary. The woman places her feet in the holsters and pulls the straps for optimum leg placement. *Voila!* Deeper, longer, more comfortable sex.

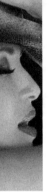

♥ **Doggystyle harness.** Rear-entry intercourse shouldn't be a pain the butt. This comfortable harness holds a woman's hips from below and raises her up high for greater G-spot stimulation—all with better balance and control for him, which also means more pleasure for both.

♥ **Ankle positioners.** For Missionary made easy, with G-spot emphasis, bring her knees to her chest and cuff her ankles into this adjustable positioner. Then let the good times roll.

♥ **G-spot positioners.** This comfortable foot-and-ankle sling gives both sets of feet extra leverage, so he can gently push off and angle accurately for her G-spot, while her hips stay perfectly positioned without rolling up and out of G-spot range.

♥ **Environmental positioners.** Get creative with what you've got. Place your hands or feet on the headboard, and push off for greater leverage, aim and deeper penetration. Or tie your lover's wrists and ankles to the bed posts. Or try a suction-cup dildo on the headboard for one more erection to play with.

Shake, Rattle & Roll!

What's the latest in hot new sex toys to enhance pleasure during intercourse? Begin salivating *now:*

♥ **Bullet vibrators.** Press this tiny vibrator onto her clitoris during penetration and she'll feel herself racing toward orgasm.

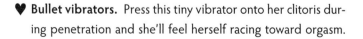

Or hold it against his testicles or taint for *his* special treat. Works wonders on each other's nipples, too.

♥ **Mini-massagers.** These discreet, powerful, lipstick-sized orgasm-makers with easy-grip handles create easier clitoral fun, and the waterproof models are always ready to delight in the shower or tub.

♥ **Hands-free vibes.** An elastic strap holds a small bullet vibe right on her clitoris, so your hands are free to roam during lovemaking. Or try a vibrating penis ring that'll delight *both* of you. Feeling adventurous? A double-vibe ring delivers some exotic testicle-tickling, too.

♥ **Him-on-her dildos.** Choose your shape for G-spot pleasuring or for girthier "hurts-so-good" thrills. For the ultimate adventure, insert one into her anus during lovemaking for a penis-dildo

> ### Dr. Sadie Sez:
> ### Pick-Up Your Toys—And Clean Them!
> Before and after each use, thoroughly clean toys with warm water and antibacterial soap or an adult toy cleanser. You can sterilize silicone dildos in boiling water or wash them on the top rack in your dishwasher, but not latex and battery-operated toys. Dry all washed toys completely before storing them.

double-penetration sensation, or try it with a strap-on for dual in-n-out motions. *Remember:* no back-and-forthing!

♥ **Her-on-him dildos.** She's the Penetrator-In-Chief with this dildo-holding strap-on harness fastened snugly around her waist, probing for orgasmic HE-spot pleasures.

Hot-To-Trot Penis Toys

If you haven't checked lately, look at how many different kinds of gadgets a guy can now look forward to:

♥ **Penis rings.** Also known as "cock rings," he straps one snugly around the base of the penis—or together with both testicles— to create harder, longer-lasting erections while helping to spout huge orgasms. Available in a variety of fabrics, rings offer features like Velcro or "release snaps" ready to open one at a time as climax nears. *Caution:* Not for men with vascular issues.

♥ **Penis extenders.** For longer length and firmer penetration, try a penis extender. Today's models are worn like condoms with soft extension heads available in different sizes to suit your needs.

♥ **Penis thickeners.** These lifelike sleeves wrap around the erect penis to create a snugger fit inside the vagina. And they allow

the head of the penis to pop out at the top, so he still enjoys lots of erotic sensations.

♥ **Penis buffers.** If he's too well-endowed for her comfort, slide on a penis buffer (aka jelly masturbator) at the base of the penis to keep from penetrating too deeply and injuring her cervix.

Backdoor Entertainment

♥ **Butt plugs.** These flared-base "can't-disappear-inside-you" plugs feel terrific during intercourse—especially the vibrating models. Just lube one up and slide it slowly inside for a sensational feeling of fullness—as well as thrilling, gripping pulsations during orgasm. Wearing a plug in her anus can narrow her vaginal canal to create tighter vaginal intercourse for him, too.

♥ **Prostate stimulators.** Try one of these prostate-seeking, orgasm-escalating toys for sensations you didn't think possible. These stimulators are curved just right to automatically excite the prostate together with the natural move-ments of intercourse—hands-free! These are also available in vibrating models. Try doing simultane-ous Kegel-squeezes for super HE-spot orgasms.

♥ **Anal T's.** These vibrating angled-to-excite toys feel like some-one else is pleasuring the prostate during intercourse. Slip one

Dr. Sadie Sez: Playing With Anal Toys? Don't Be A Butt-Head!

Rule One: Use lube. Always. *Rule Two:* Insert and extract toys slowly. *Rule Three:* Choose toys that don't trap bacteria, such as non-porous silicone or glass (or roll a condom over latex or rubber). *Rule Four:* No back-and-forthing between anus and vagina. *Rule Five:* Practice the safety tips in the Appendix.

in, turn it on, and let its vibrations do all the work, while you work her.

Slippery Sensations

Sex lubricants now come in many different varieties—try a few till you find the feel that slips it to you best.

♥ **Water-based lubes.** From watery "pour-it-on" liquids to thick "ooze-it-on" gels, this type of lube is compatible with condoms and every type of sex toy. It comes in lots of exotic flavors for oral slurping, too. Gels last longer, so be sure to replenish thinner lubes more often. Clean-up is easy and stain-free, and washes right off everything, including you.

♥ **Silicone-based lubes.** This type of lube is longer-lasting and super slippery. Great for anal play and perfect for sex in a shower,

hot tub, or pool because it stays slippery, even in water. *However, it will create a slip-hazard if it drips on bathroom tiles.* Be careful. Requires a little extra effort to wash off.

♥ **Lube shooters.** Don't order one at happy hour, but these single-use lube-tubes will make you very happy. Squeeze one deep inside the vagina or anus, and you'll enjoy total slipperiness when and where you need it. Try a silicone shooter before underwater intercourse, or for longer-lasting anal play.

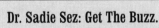

Dr. Sadie Sez: Get The Buzz.

To learn more about the joys of toys, including selection, techniques, and safety, feel free to pick up a copy of my book, *TOYGASMS! The Insider's Guide to Sex Toys and Techniques* at *ticklekitty.com*.

Appendix: Safety First— Protect Yourself

This book is about pleasure, positions, orgasms and sex.

It's also about health, honesty, safety and self-protection.

No human on the planet is immune from today's sexually transmitted infections (STIs). You can catch one or more from intimate sexual contact with someone who's already infected, either through vaginal, oral or anal sex, or even genital rubbing with no penetration.

What's the difference between an STI and an STD (sexually transmitted disease)? The term STI has a broader meaning; a person may be infected (through viruses or bacteria), and has the potential to infect others, while showing no signs of disease. The infected person may not feel sick, or even be aware of the infection. An STD is an STI that has begun to exhibit the symptoms of disease. Because our focus is on prevention, this book uses the term STI to epmphasize that you can become infected from a sexual partner, *even if that person shows no symptoms.*

STIs can last a lifetime, damage your relationships, cause sterility and birth defects, and lead to tragic illness and death. Sobering? Yes. Is there something you can do? Yes.

Practice Safer Sex—Here's How

Those who take the safest route—total abstinence from sex with anyone else—probably aren't reading this book (but if you're peeking, pick up a nice vibrating sextoy or two, along with some slippery sex lube. Masturbating is perfectly safe!).

The next safest option is total monogamy. This means you promise to be 100 percent faithful to your lover—and you both keep that promise. No cheating, no needle sharing. You'll still need to practice birth control to reduce the risk of unwanted pregnancy.

But what if you're in non-committed relationships, or engaging in casual, or "friends with benefits" sex? There's really only one way to decrease your chances of contracting or transmitting STIs— or even ending up with an unwanted pregnancy: *practice safer sex—each and every time.*

The good news: you're mostly safe kissing, licking, nibbling, sucking and massaging your lover everywhere but on the private parts (but you can catch cold sores if your partner has them on the mouth). And you're mostly safe bringing your partner to orgasm

through Outercourse (chapter 15), as long as you keep your partner's body fluids from entering your body, either through an orifice or a cut in your skin. (This includes semen, pre-come, vaginal fluids, blood, and—take a deep breath—discharge from sores caused by STIs.)

Steps To Safer Sex— Easier Than You Think

1. **Know your partner.** Lower your risk by limiting your number of sexual partners, and skipping anonymous and casual sex. It's okay to ask a partner about his or her sexual history. If a new lover pulls out a condom without you ever asking, that's a good sign. If he resists a "glove"—then no love!

2. **Practice monogamy.** This means being completely faithful. Start with testing to be sure you're both free of any hidden STIs from the get-go. If you have the slightest doubt your partner may not be completely monogamous, insist on protection.

3. **Use latex condoms.** Without fail, roll a fresh latex condom over the penis before it ever touches the vagina, mouth or anus. Roll them over sextoys, too. And always use sex lubes that are "latex-compatible," such as water-based varieties.

4. **Store condoms wisely.** Keep a fresh supply on hand. Don't leave them in the heat, glovebox or wallet. Never re-use them. And always toss them after their expiration date. If you open one that looks or smells bad, don't use it.

5. **Use dams, gloves and cots.** Before engaging in cunnilingus or analingus, place a latex dam or a large sheet of plastic wrap over the vulva or anus so the mouth and lips never touch the skin. Don't invert them, and never re-use them. For fingerplay, wear a latex glove or "finger cot," a snug latex cover that rolls onto your finger.

6. **Apply sex lubricant.** And plenty of it. It's inexpensive, feels good and essential for anal play.

7. **Stay sober.** Drinking alcohol and taking recreational drugs weaken your resolve, lessen your ability to communicate, and make it tougher to focus on putting on a condom correctly. Know when to say "when."

8. **Wash up.** Before anyone touches anything, wash hands with antibacterial soap and warm water. This includes fingers, sextoys and yourselves. Don't introduce germs from the outside world onto and into your most sensitive private parts. If he's uncircumcised, encourage him to wash under his foreskin—every day.

9. **Clean your sextoys.** Before and after each use, wash each sextoy with water and antibacterial soap or an adult toy cleanser. You can sterilize silicone and glass dildos in boiling water or wash them on the top rack in your dishwasher. Dry your washed sextoys completely before storing them, or for the safest results, let them air-dry.

10. **Be a neat lover.** Toss all used condoms in the trash. Throw after-sex wipe-up towels right into the hamper. Keep a container of good disposable wipes near the bed. Wash all bedsheets after you've "used" them, too.

Take Extra Care For Anal Sex

11. **Single dip only.** Once you've committed to the back door—the vagina and mouth are off limits till after penis and hands are thoroughly washed, or you'll risk introducing germs that can lead to infection.

12. **Get slippery.** Unlike the vagina, the rectum is delicate and dry, with no natural lubrication to glide the penis inside. You MUST squeeze on the lube—in large, generous amounts. And don't even *think* about using quick-to-lose-its-slip saliva.

13. **Choose and use sextoys carefully.** Sextoys designed for anal play come with a wide, flared base or extra-long handle for you to grip, so they're unable to slip inside and disappear. Never back-and-forth a sextoy between orifices. Always apply lube, insert gently, follow the natural curve of the rectum, and stop immediately if there's ever any pain.

14. **Eliminate rough edges.** Some sextoys arrive from the factory with rough edges and seams that are dangerous if inserted. Before first use, examine every sextoy closely by running your fingertips over the entire surface, and file smooth any roughness or sharpness you find. While you're at it, file your fingernails smooth, too.

15. **Set up barriers.** Roll a smooth spermicide-free latex condom over the penis, as well as over any sextoys you plan to insert. If inserting fingers, wear latex gloves or finger cots. Place a latex dam or large sheet of plastic wrap between any tongue-to-anus stimulation—or cut a fresh latex condom lengthwise and lay it flat. Never invert or re-use any latex barriers—always toss them out.

16. **Pee when finished.** Urinate immediately after sex to flush your urethra of any bacteria you might have picked up, and send them rushing out before they can work their way in.

How To Guarantee UN-Safe Sex

NEVER try any of these moves—no matter what anyone tells you:

✔ **Never fall for "I'll pull out."** This UNsafe practice of withdrawing the penis from the vagina, mouth or anus before ejaculation can easily lead to STIs or pregnancy. "Pre-come" almost always leaks out before his orgasm. Always roll a condom over the penis before any penetration.

✔ **Never use Nonoxynol-9.** Once thought to prevent the spread of the HIV virus, scientific testing has revealed this lubricant actually *increases* the risk of transmission. Do not use N-9 lubricant or condoms coated with N-9 lubricant.

✔ **Never use household lubricants.** Slippery liquids and gels found around the house are awful for intercourse and can destroy condoms. Never use petroleum jelly, vegetable shortening, cooking oils, lip balm or anything slippery that isn't specifically designed for sex.

✔ **Never insert objects not designed for sex.** Although they may have the right shape, never insert hairbrushes, fruits, vegetables, bottles, or cans into the vagina or anus—they can be dangerous and difficult to extract if lost inside.

Solutions To Safer Sex WHAT IFs

WHAT IF you give a handjob without a condom? You're safe, as long as you don't have any fresh cuts, open sores or cracks from chapping on your hands. Until your hands are healed, put a condom on him when giving handjobs, or wear a latex glove you can lube on the outside.

WHAT IF you forgot to use birth control—or the condom broke? You can take emergency contraception (EC) within 120 hours (5 days) after unprotected intercourse, but the sooner, the better. But remember: EC does not protect you from STIs, nor should it be used in lieu of birth control.

WHAT IF either of you is allergic to latex condoms? It may be the latex, or the spermicide already on the condom. Try a condom without spermicide, or a polyurethane condom instead, but do **not** use condoms made of lambskin, since they will not block the transmission of many STIs.

WHAT IF he's uncomfortable in condoms? Try switching styles or brands—you can now find latex condoms in all different shapes, sizes and thicknesses, from extra large to snugger fit to wider at the tip. Test-drive a few and find a new favorite.

WHAT IF you want to share a sextoy? Don't. But if it's going to happen in the heat of passion, roll a fresh condom on it each

Dr. Sadie Sez: Why Must This All Sound So Dire?

STIs are serious business, yet the threat is all-too-easy to brush off when the opportunity for casual sex presents itself in the shape of a handsome stranger or a willing babe. While much of this information does not pertain to you when you're in a faithfully monogamous relationship, it DOES pertain to you 100 percent if you are sexually active with a partner or partners of unknown sexual histories—no matter what they might tell you. Protect yourself. Everything you need to know to preserve your health is in your hands.

time it's going to be enjoyed by a different person. Then clean the sextoy thoroughly with antibacterial soap or adult toy cleanser between uses.

What Are The Symptoms Of STIs?

Each type of infection has its own symptoms, but the most common include:

- ✔ Unusual discharge from penis or vagina

- ✔ Warts, sores, itching or burning in the genital area

- ✔ A burning sensation during urination

- ✔ Anal itching, soreness or bleeding

If this is happening to you, or you suspect you may have caught an STI, see your physician immediately. Do not be embarrassed or shy, and do not wait—the sooner you act, the better off you'll be.

What Kinds Of STIs Are Out There?

Unfortunately, there are over 20 different types of sexually transmitted infections you can catch during unprotected sex—and it takes only one slip-up to put yourself at risk. You are not limited to catching one at a time—a partner infected with several could pass them *all* along to you in one act of unprotected sex.

STIs Can Either Be Bacterial Or Viral:

Bacterial STIs. Can be treated and often cured with antibiotics, so the sooner you see your doctor, the easier it will be for the cure to work. Bacterial STIs include syphilis, gonorrhea and chlamydia.

Viral STIs. Can be treated, but not cured with today's medicine, and you will have it the rest of your life. The sooner you see your doctor, the more effectively it can be controlled. Viral STIs include HIV/AIDS, genital herpes, genital warts, human papillomavirus (HPV) and hepatitis B.

Left untreated, STIs can lead to serious complications, including liver failure, cancers, neurological difficulties, and even death.

Although both men and women are at risk, the burden of infection can be more severe for women:

✔ A pregnant woman can pass her STI to the baby before and during the baby's birth.

✔ A woman can become infertile if an STI goes undetected and untreated over a period of time.

✔ HPV, an all-too-common STI, is now recognized as the major cause of cervical cancer.

What To Do?

Millions of people unknowingly carry and transmit STIs to sex partners, either because they have no symptoms, or simply choose to ignore them. The only way you can know if you or your partner has an STI is to get tested at a reputable clinic or doctor's office. Don't put it off.

Your best weapons against STIs? Use protection. Say no to casual hook-ups. Know your partner. Stay monogamous. And get regular checkups.

Learn More About Protecting Yourself

CDC Centers for Disease Control and Prevention

http://www.cdc.gov/std

Call 1-800-CDC-INFO for information and referrals to STD clinics

American Social Health Association

http://www.ashastd.org

National Women's Health Information Center

http://www.4women.gov/faq/stdsgen.htm

Planned Parenthood

http://www.plannedparenthood.org

AfterPlay

This isn't the end, it's a beginning.

By mastering the positions and techniques of lovemaking, you'll feel your deeper emotional connection evolving, too—flowing with intimacy, creativity, generosity, pleasure, love.

Think sensually. Act joyously. Touch slowly. Laugh freely. Orgasm lavishly. And celebrate all the new love and passion in your life.

X's and O's

Dr. Sadie

Dr. Sadie Allison

P.S. Please feel free to share your learning and loving experiences with me, and let me know how this book has inspired and intensified your lovemaking. Your complete confidentiality is assured, of course. Write to me at *ticklekitty.com*, or Tickle Kitty, 3701 Sacramento Street #107, San Francisco, CA 94118 USA.

Dr. Sadie's
Pleasure Position Index

Find *Your* New Favorite Position:

Special Thanks

A deep, ecstatic, joyous THANK YOU to my all-star publishing team. I bless the sweet angel on my shoulder who led me to each of you:

Rich Lippman—Wordmaster *extraordinaire*. Thank you for your work on this amazing, accessible, super-creative fourth book.

Steve Lee—Illustrator *exceptionale*. Your instructional drawings play so seductively.

Chris Hall—Text designer *impressivo*. Your beautiful layouts bring this book to life.

Todd Gallopo—Cover designer *magnifico*. Your superb concepts are truly eye-opening.

Thanks to my close friends and peers who always support of my creative endeavors:

Mark S., Lisa M., Elizabeth T., Bo P., Jenna M., Joanna M., Danalynn D., Sara R., Shelly C. & Mike R., Dana W., Vajra H., Laura H., E. Moy, Sue J., Randy G., Ted M., Barbara L., Ian K.

And to my family—thank you for your strength and love:

My beautiful mother: This one's for *YOU*, **Mom**!

The best friend anyone could ever dream for: **Kristin L.**

My sweet little sister who loves unconditionally: **Jazmin J.**

The coolest brother with the biggest heart: **Jason J.**

The greatest little girl in the world, my daughter: **Sienna**

About the Author

When you need answers about lovemaking, look to **Dr. Sadie Allison**, founder and CEO of Tickle Kitty, Inc., and *ticklekitty.com*.

Dr. Sadie is a leading authority on human sexuality today, and author of the award-winning bestsellers *Tickle His Pickle*, *TOYGASMS!* and *Tickle Your Fancy*. She appears frequently on TV and radio, including *E! Entertainment Television*, *Talk Sex with Sue Johanson*, Dr. Drew's *Loveline* and the *Bob & Tom Show*. She is a sought-after speaker, and is often quoted in national magazines, such as *Cosmopolitan*, *Redbook* and *Men's Health*.

She's a Licensed Doctor of Human Sexuality, having earned her degree in 2005 from the Institute for Advanced Study of Human Sexuality. She's also a member of the American Association of Sex Educators, Counselors & Therapists (AASECT). Her Tickle Kitty brand of sex-help books, sensual pleasure kits and sex lubricants enable her to assist more individuals and couples find greater joys in sexual pleasure.

Dr. Sadie was born, raised, and still resides in San Francisco, California, where she's raising her beautiful daughter.

Arise
&shine!

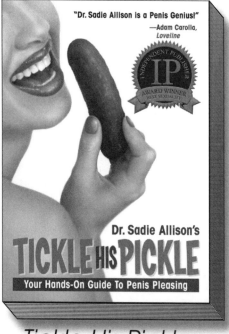

Tickle His Pickle

Every woman's hands-on guide
to penis pleasing.
by Dr. Sadie Allison

Available at bookstores, fine sex boutiques and pleasure parties.
Or online at ticklekitty.com

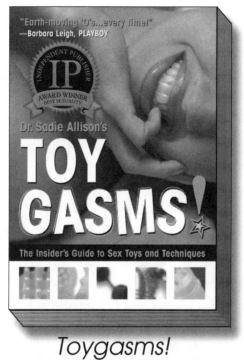

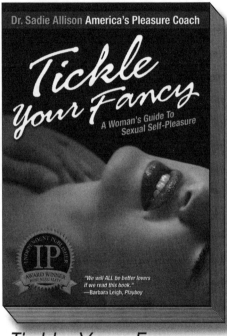